Teach Baby to Sleep

The Ultimate Guide to Building Good Sleeping habits from birth to One Year

by
Ines Zdelar

Published by Mabel and Stanley Publishing – Dec 2024

Disclaimer

The advice given in this book is based on the author's knowledge and experience gained over many years. Please be aware that this advice serves purely as a guide and will be different for every individual family and baby.

The content is no substitute for medical advice and families should always seek guidance from a medical professional if they feel worried or unsure.

The author cannot accept responsibility for any results or consequences of using the book content and ultimate responsibility for babies' safety and wellbeing rests firmly with the parent or guardian in charge.

Results may vary according to family and babies needs especially if there are medical or developmental needs in existence.

Get in Touch

Follow me on Instagram for news of upcoming courses and great tips and advice for you and your baby.

@ines_zdelar.sleepcoach

Contents

Chapter 1 9

What I Believe in and How to Navigate This Book 9

Chapter 2 23

Understanding Sleep 23

Chapter 3 35

Realistic Expectations About Sleep 35

Chapter 4 45

Understanding Newborns 45

Chapter 5 57

Comfort and Feeding 57

Sleep and Feeding Connection 57

Chapter 6 73

Welcoming Your Newborn 73

Chapter 7 103

Baby Sleep (4-6 Months) 103

Chapter 8 121

Baby Sleep (7-9 Months) 121

Chapter 9 135

Baby Sleep (10-12 Months) 135

Chapter 10 147

Prioritising Mothers' Well Being 147

Chapter 11 157

Father's Role 157

Chapter 12 169

Connection and Well-being Techniques That I Swear by 169

REVIEWS FOR TEACHING BABY TO SLEEP 179

About the Author 181

"There is a time
for
many words,
and there is also
a time
for sleep."

Homer

Chapter 1

What I Believe in and How to Navigate This Book

Introduction

I was born in Croatia and moved to the UK when I turned 18. I always knew that my calling was in childcare from a young age. When I arrived in the UK I began my childcare journey as a nanny in London. And the rest is history. I now have 25 years of experience working with families and children in various roles. I've taught in Montessori nurseries, and I am also a qualified swimming instructor for babies and children.

I've always been drawn to babies, and always fascinated by the babies' ability to learn, which led me to become a postnatal maternity nurse. The maternity nursing role helped me better understand mothers and babies and their unique connection.

While working as a maternity nurse, I saw how sleep deprivation can have an impact in everyday life in every family. I have experienced sleep deprivation myself and started to dive deep into the science of sleep. I became interested in sleep and its healing properties. This is how the 'family sleep coach' was born.

I started to implement my experience while I was in sleep recovery myself using methods that worked for me every single time. These methods do not originate from me. I like to call it mix and match, having studied and applied them all but only keeping the ones that had a significant impact and improved my sleep.

My approach is gentle, no-tears, but I put immense importance on consistency, patience and trust. There is one more thing I truly believes is the key to success; start them early.

My book is a gentle step by step guide for new parents, where at first you are starting them young, very young. Week by week I will be offering practical advice and tasks to follow, to create a happy little sleeper by age one. I am warm and compassionate, and I like to empower parents to establish healthy daily sleep routines from day one, not only for their baby but for themselves.

Why Did I Write This Book?

In this book you will find all sorts of information that will help you as a first-time mother. It is all the knowledge that I have gained over the last 25 years in the childcare industry. This book is a guide and if you follow the roadmap of the tasks, step by step, age appropriate, you will have a happy little sleeper by age one.

Will This Work?

This will work, but you need to remember, there is no magic wand, no overnight miracle and no quick fix.
For this to work you will have to put in place the schedule and do it every single day. Sadly, I can't do it for you, nobody can. There will be times when you will want to give up, when you are tired and overwhelmed, but if you keep your eye on the prize and keep doing it

repeatedly, your message will be clear. Your baby will feel safe with you and they will know what follows.

My Core Beliefs

My beliefs come from a process I have been developing and changing through the years; always improving and trying to give the best to my clients.

My approach is holistic, that means I am not focusing only on one thing. I am involving body, mind and spirit. These three things need to be in place to be able to create balance in your life, your wellbeing, as well as your baby's.

From my experience everything starts with you and your beliefs. If you are not ready to step into this process, your baby will also not be ready. Please don't expect your baby to do what you don't believe in. If you think he or she can do it, they will do it.

Here is how I back up this; when you believe in something, you will have more patience and will do it again and again, until you figure out what is the best way of doing it. But if you start making excuses. Guess what? They won't do it.

They might not be able to do it today but that doesn't mean they won't be able to do it tomorrow. Believe in yourself and believe in your baby.

Consistency is also one of the key elements to creating habits that will unlock peaceful sleep. There is always space for flexibility; there needs to be as we are not robots. Consistency is the backbone of my beliefs. Consistency gives your baby a sense of security, leaving no space for confusion.

Patience is another skill I would like you to activate in this process. Patience will allow you to be kind to yourself when things are not going according to plan. And yes, sometimes things will get worse before they get better. But knowing this will also help you to progress on this journey.

I believe in instinct, that inner voice, called intuition. This should be your guide, your compass in navigating parenting. Nobody understands your baby's needs more than you. Advice from others can be helpful, but always align what your heart tells you.

I believe that your baby is always talking to you. If you turn on that intuition, connect deeply, approach sleep with love, and respect the natural rhythms of their development, magic will happen. You will learn how to read their cues; you will create awareness that will flow between you and your baby.

I also believe in energy. Babies are remarkably attuned to emotions and the atmosphere around them. A calm, relaxed parent often leads to a calm and comfortable, happy baby.

I believe that power lays in a strong foundation for healthy sleep from day one. I am not talking about rigid schedules but gently introducing positive sleep associations. Doing this allows your baby to catch a natural rhythm that aligns with their needs, making sleep a loving part of their life.

I believe that by applying everything step by step, by their first birthday, they'll likely develop a love for sleep and their bed.

I believe that every family is different, and every parenting journey is personal, it should be that way, your family values and beliefs will shape your baby's path. There is no right or wrong, just different perspectives on parenthood.

This book might not align with every parenting style. This book will offer support and practical guidance for those seeking alternative methods to co-sleeping.

I believe that there is something powerful that happens when your child sleeps independently. When you give them love and security but letting them rest in their own space.

Understanding Co-Sleeping and its Impact

The safest place for your baby to sleep is in their own separate sleep space, on a flat and clear surface, to reduce the risk of SIDS (sudden infant death syndrome). It is the safest guideline backed up by The Lullaby Trust.

As someone who has done lots of research on sleep, I need to address co-sleeping. Co-sleeping has become more popular but has left parents divided. Some parents love the idea of co-sleeping and will do it, while others are not that keen on it.

What is Co-Sleeping?

Co-sleeping is a practice where parents and children share a sleeping space.

Let's see what science says about co-sleeping.
Some studies suggest that co-sleeping in the early years can lead to clinginess and dependence in

children. It is often linked to the constant physical closeness and immediate response to a child's needs, potentially impacting their ability to self-soothe and develop independence.

However, it's important to note that scientific research in this area is complex and affected by various cultural, social and individual factors.

While keeping that in mind, let me share my journey, which shapes my perspective on co-sleeping.

I was a co-sleeper. My mother was a single parent who loved me deeply and always wanted only the best for me. We co-slept throughout my childhood and even into my teens.

When I was little, I loved it. It felt so safe and happy. It was such a good feeling to snuggle every night next to my mum and hug her, knowing that she was always so close to me.

But then I entered my teen years, my own strong feelings became involved. I wanted to have my own personal space, where I could be independent and find my own identity.

I knew that this closeness meant so much to my mother. Watching her being so happy with me sleeping next to her, I continued to share a bed while putting my feelings aside and suppressing my needs for independence.

I have never talked about this before. Even though I loved being close to my mother, later in life it became a compromise. A compromise that was made because of the love towards my mum, but it has left scars. I became an incredibly needy child, always seeking attention, mostly from people close to me. I have had this emotional dependence carried into my teenage years. It manifested itself as a clinginess and possessiveness.

It was a hard time for me; I didn't like how much I depended on others.

I worked hard to get out of this behaviour pattern, the only good thing was that I was aware of it.

When I became aware of it to the point that it started to bother me, I made a big step. I moved to another country when I was 18.

I stepped out of my comfort zone, my safe place. But this move opened my eyes, and I found ways how to overcome all the issues. I stepped into independence and self-discovery, away, far away, from the life I knew.

While I am sharing this story, I don't want you to paint the wrong picture about my mum. She did her best. I wanted to share this story to show you that co-sleeping can have an impact. I am aware that lots of parents and children might find themselves doing it.

When I reflect on this, I wish I had expressed my need for independence earlier. If I had vocalised it, Mum would have made sure that I had personal space earlier. It was a tough one as I craved that individual space while also wanting to keep that closeness with my mother.

While telling my story, I see a connection with science. Deep down I believe that co-sleeping is not needed to feel close to your baby.

This story should send you the message, sometimes love can be smothering. And I am sure you will have lots of decisions to make on this journey through parenthood.

If you're a parent who strongly believes in co-sleeping, this book might not be for you. This book is for parents who are ready to introduce independent sleeping from day one.

Navigating this Book: Tips on How to use the Book

I have written this book to be your helpful guide and companion in your parenting sleep journey from birth to one year. I understand that parenting can be challenging, so I have created this book to offer you the support and guidance you need at every step to get you and your baby better sleep.

To make the most of this book, read it in the order of your baby's growth, following the guiding arrows that indicate the information relevant to each month. I have designed the book to help you avoid feeling overwhelmed. Each chapter builds on the previous one so that you and your baby can adjust to new changes gradually.

As you read through each chapter, I will offer new tips and techniques for enhancing your routine and making it flow seamlessly.

Practical Guidance and Support for New Parents

I understand that a mother's intuition is a superpower that should be listened to; I have developed it not by giving birth but by observing babies closely, by watching them and their parents interacting, by learning from my own experiences, by being there for parents and children when they needed me the most. There is no greater achievement in life than when you look at your little kiddies growing into beautiful human beings.

Dear Mamma, remember to celebrate every success, no matter how small and to focus on what you've achieved rather than what you haven't. Give yourself that pat on the back and be proud of what you have accomplished each day. You are always doing your best, don't let anyone tell you differently.

The most important thing is to stay grateful; you have been blessed, look at your baby, you have created a new life, you can do this!

There is so much pressure on parenthood today. Parenthood and childcare were far simpler only ten years ago. But with this fast-paced lifestyle, and social media promoting the desire to be perfect in all aspects of life, pressure on parents is huge.

The reason I wrote this book is to help first-time mothers decide what is best for their baby by giving them information and then guiding them step by step, rather than giving them lots of chunks of information that they don't know how to action. With this book I wanted to guide every first-time parent, like we are in the same room. I want them to feel my presence. To feel empowered, to feel safe.

We all have read lots of books and know how we should do things, but how we apply this knowledge is the key to success. With this book you don't have to do much; just relax and take it one day at a time, reading only the chapters and sections of the book that apply to your baby's age.

Building a Connection and Understanding First-Time Mothers

As a new mother, you've embarked on a journey you've eagerly anticipated for nine months. The moment you hold your newborn in your arms, a mix of emotions floods over you - confusion, overwhelm, and love like never before.

You are happy to be able to go home and enjoy time with your little one, but the question rising in your head is: Is that it? They are just letting me home without pointers, without a manual. And there and then, you realise that you oversee this helpless little baby of yours for the next 18 years.

That moment changes everything. You change. You feel a shift, a surge of love every time you look at your little one. You now love, and feel love, and see it before you. You are now a mother, and you are complete.

On the other side you feel lost, lonely, forgetful, confused. It is everything you have ever imagined and more but on the other side, no one could prepare you for it; you have read the books but when you hold that baby and it starts crying, you would do anything for them to stop crying, but hear me now, not all the cries are bad crying, it's your baby's only way to communicate with you, to regulate, to express their emotions. You don't understand the cues just yet, but soon, you will understand each other, and soon, you will know what your baby is telling you.

Dear Mummy, don't worry—you've got this. The first few weeks may not be easy, but they are a valuable learning experience for both you and your baby. Your little one is just as confused as you are, having spent the last nine months in your tummy. Now, they're learning about the world, and they've chosen you as their guide, their Mummy.

When the baby is born, so is the mother; you have never experienced this, so the two of you are stepping into the unknown. Needing each other to grow and to bloom. Enjoy this time. It is when the connection happens, and you take all the time to pay attention to what your baby is saying. Oh, how lovely that can be; you and your baby are in the same shoes, nobody knows anything about that other person, both sides start fresh, and you are both learning simultaneously. While the bond that you have is something out of the ordinary.

“Sleep is the best meditation.”

Dalai Lama

Chapter 2

Understanding Sleep

What is Sleep?

Sleep is a natural and essential part of life. It's the time when your body and mind rest and recharge. During sleep, we go through different stages that help us feel refreshed and ready for the next day.

When we go to sleep, lots of processes are happening. We don't just close our eyes and fall asleep until morning when we open our eyes and are awake. In sleep, during the night, we go through cycles. Sleeping involves cycles with different stages of sleep, from drowsiness to light sleep and eventually deep sleep. Our bodies might still look like we are resting and restoring our energy, but sleep is an active state, crucial for physical and mental wellbeing. There are two main types of sleep:

Non-REM Sleep (Non-Rapid Eye Movement Sleep)

Non-REM sleep is the deep, restful sleep where your brain takes a break. Newborns will spend 50% in REM and 50% in Non-REM and that is why it is sometimes difficult to wake up newborns. Adults spend around 75% of the night in non-REM sleep. During this time, blood flows to the muscles, tissues grow or get repaired, hormones needed for growth are released, and white blood cells are produced to boost the immune system. In this stage, you will breathe steadily and deeply, and it will be harder to wake up. Non-REM sleep cycles go through various stages, each deeper than the last, before transitioning into REM sleep. Here is one important thing to remember, non-REM sleep is not fully developed until your baby is around 4 months old.

REM Sleep (Rapid Eye Movement Sleep)

REM sleep is essential for brain development, it is a stage of sleep when dreams happen. In this stage our eyes move behind our eyelids while we are dreaming. Brain activity in this stage is very similar to brain activity of an awake person. You will spend around 25% of your sleep in REM sleep. During REM sleep, the body rests, extra blood flows to the brain and we process everything we have seen and heard during the day. REM sleep plays a key role in memory consolidation and cognitive function. Since REM sleep is so crucial for mental rejuvenation, we spend a significant portion of our sleep time in this stage. Because REM sleep is so important for development, young babies spend a lot of time in REM sleep. It remains important throughout our lives, through childhood and adolescence and into adulthood.

Have you ever wondered what makes your baby fall asleep at night?

The answer lies in two powerful sleep regulators: melatonin and cortisol. Let's delve into the fascinating world of these sleep hormones and understand their role in your baby's sleep patterns.

Melatonin

Primarily known as the sleep hormone, melatonin's function regulates sleep and tells your body that it's nighttime and it is time to go to bed. When your baby goes to sleep, and for you as well, it is essential for melatonin levels to be high. Luckily, you can influence this by having a great, predictable bath time and bedtime routine. For the body to start producing melatonin, you will need darkness, so keep the lights dimmed around bathtime, and avoid any blue light like TV or screens. The good news is that your baby's melatonin will naturally increase when they reach 3 months; this is a sweet spot and an ideal opportunity to establish a good bath time and bedtime routine and encourage positive sleep habits and association.

Cortisol

Also known as the stress hormone, cortisol is created when the body is overtired or sleep deprived. If your or your baby's cortisol levels are high, they will find it difficult to fall asleep. This can lead to nighttime waking and early rising, disrupting both yours and your baby's sleep. For that reason, it's crucial for babies to have good daytime naps. Think of it this way: Too much cortisol is like you have just had a dose of caffeine, making it hard to relax and fall asleep.

Sleep Cycles

It's natural for healthy newborns to wake up when they are hungry, uncomfortable, or no longer in need of sleep. As your baby reaches 3 to 4 months, their sleep pattern naturally matures, transitioning into cycles of light and deep sleep. At night, these cycles, lasting between 40 and 50 minutes, end with a gentle awakening or arousal, marking the end of each cycle.

With the knowledge that sleep cycles will lengthen and melatonin levels will rise around this age, parents can look forward to longer stretches of sleep for their baby at night. Especially the first part of the night.

It's crucial to remember that the Circadian rhythm is also maturing at this age. This body clock plays a significant role in sleep, wakefulness, rest, hunger, activity, body temperature, and hormones. Therefore, babies at this age respond well to routine, which helps to harmonise these rhythms. This period presents a wonderful opportunity for parents to guide their baby and establish a healthy routine, including regular feeding times, nap times, a predictable bath time, bedtime routine, and encouraging self-soothing.

Sleep is a natural process, but we have lost connection with natural methods in this busy world. Quite often, we as adults don't listen to our bodies telling us to slow down and rest; we push through that tired window as there is one more thing that needs to be crossed off your to-do list. But we need to realise that missing the sleep window opportunity is like missing that last train; another one is not coming until morning. So, we get ready to sleep overtired and then can't fall asleep as cortisol stress hormone levels are too high. Or we fall asleep and wake up very tired. This is because we have never entered deep restorative sleep. This is an expected behaviour that we all do. Me included.

If we as adults are disconnected from natural rhythms of sleep, how can we teach our little ones to sleep?

Here is the harsh truth: sleep is natural to all of us but is a learned skill. It has nothing to do with luck. You are the only one who can help your baby learn it from day one.
Be responsive and gentle, offer reassurance and comfort, and follow your baby's needs. Even when you cover all your baby's needs, you can still guide them and clearly tell them that nighttime is for sleeping. Babies are tuned in and pick up your signals and energy.

Rest assured, babies who are guided to develop healthy sleep habits from an early stage, will continue to be content sleepers throughout their lives.

Sleep Environment

I would like to address how important the sleep environment is to optimise your newborn's sleep as well as yours. A relaxing environment is crucial for a good night's sleep. When you as a new Mum, are aware how to optimise sleep by making your sleep space more soothing and suitable for good rest, this will reflect on your mood and the mood of your baby, when awake.

Scientists have found that the more the sleep environment is like the environment in the womb then it is more likely that they will fall asleep quickly, and the duration and quality of sleep will improve.

Let us focus on how each aspect of your bedroom setting will influence the way you and your baby sleep:

Light and Darkness

Darkness plays an important part in linking sleep

cycles. Darkness also promotes melatonin production and enhances feelings of sleepiness and relaxation. Your baby will start with melatonin production when they reach 6 weeks old. Until then, they will be guided by you.

I am not saying that your baby won't be able to sleep in a room with a light, but they will sleep the best in the darkness. Light often stimulates the baby's brain and tells our body to produce the alert hormone, cortisol. This is the reason why I always advise darkness both for naps during the day and sleep at night.

Night Feedings

What do you do at night? you ask me. I would highly recommend a night lamp for your baby's night feeds; a lamp that doesn't light the whole room, just gives you enough light to see what you are doing. The lamp light should be warm, yellow, orange or a red glow.

I love, love, love the Himalayan Salt Lamp; it has the most amazing, warm glow and enough visibility. You can also leave them on for the duration of night, in case you must check on your baby. Himalayan Salt Lamps are not only perfect lamps for creating warm ambience during the feeds, but they also have so many benefits, like improving air quality, improving moods... more about Himalayan salt lamps later in the book.

Blue Light

At night and just before bed, significantly disrupts yours and your baby's sleep. Blue light promotes alertness and performance. When you are using blue light (televisions, smartphones, tablets, computers) you are suppressing the production of melatonin, a sleep hormone. Using blue light will keep you awake and take longer for you to fall asleep and can delay your circadian rhythms.

Not all the blue light is bad. Mostly the blue light from electronics relates to sleep challenges. While natural blue light like the sun helps regulate your wake and sleep cycles.

Temperature

The ideal temperature of the room that will also be the safest for your baby, can vary from 16 - 20 C'. Use light bedding, swaddle, or if the baby is older, please use only a well-fitted sleeping bag. Make sure that your baby won't be too hot or too cold and use a room thermometer where your baby sleeps. Cooler temperatures will help lower the body temperature making it easier to experience deeper sleep. Melatonin production is enhanced in lower temperatures and that will lead to better sleep quality for you and your baby.

Quiet Room

When your baby is sleeping in a noisy room, their sleep can be disrupted. Babies are particularly sensitive to sound. Noises in the sleep environment can overstimulate them and lower their ability to fall asleep. Complete silence is not always achievable in our busy noisy world. That is ok, because babies really like soft, consistent, soothing background sounds. In today's world known as white noise.

White Noise

White noise is a consistent noise, it can block out other noises and babies can fall asleep so much faster with a white noise in the background. I would highly recommend getting one of the white noise machines. Some of them have a heartbeat setting, newborns might find this setting very comforting as it is mimicking the womb noise. If you choose to go for a white noise, make sure that every time your little one goes to sleep you play the same sound, this will instinctively give them signs it is time for sleep.

Tidy Room

This is the one that not many people will mention. But keeping your sleeping environment tidy will help you sleep better. Creating your own sleep sanctuary will add that calmness to you and then reflect on your baby. Untidiness is linked to higher cortisol levels and that can lead to making you feel anxious which will affect your ability to fall asleep.

Bedtime Routine

A bedtime routine is a process of calming activities that signal to your baby that it is time for sleep. Bedtime routine signals to your baby that the day has now ended, and it is time to wind down; it is the perfect time for you and your baby to connect.

The bedtime routine special formula that works every time is: calm and present parent, and simple steps that you will follow every night in the same order. Bedtime routine shouldn't be longer than 30 min. Your baby's bedtime routine allows you to use all this sleep association as a cue.

Newborn (0-4 months) Bedtime Routine Example:

Dimmed lights
Bath
Nappy change
Massage
Pyjamas
Feeding
Swaddle/Sleeping Bag
Lights off
Cuddle and Bedtime Song
White noise
Sleep in a Cot or Moses Basket

Baby (5-12months) Bedtime Routine Example

Bath
Nappy Change
Massage
Pyjamas Feeding
Sleeping Bag
Book
Lights off
Cuddle and Bedtime song
White noise
Sleep in a Cot

"The problem is not our babies, the problem is our expectations."

@sleepspaceau

Chapter 3

Realistic Expectations About Sleep

You know that saying, "sleeping like a baby" ... I am sorry dear Mummy, but I am about to burst your bubble. Babies are not good sleepers, they wake up often, they are very noisy and move a lot in their sleep. "Sleeping like a baby, " is often used by people who have never had a child.

Parenting is a new amazing chapter where you go all in and there is no way out, it's a one-way street. You will enjoy this chapter so much, but I don't want to sugar coat it as there are going to be rough patches, of not sleeping and crying. That is why I think it is useful to give you a realistic picture about how your sleep will be broken, especially in the first few weeks. It's important to get ready and mentally prepare for it.

Parenthood is the time when your life will be turned upside down, especially as you have a lack of sleep. There will be sleep progression, which is the gradual improvement in your baby's sleep patterns, then regression caused by developmental milestones, which are periods when your baby's sleep may be disrupted due to growth and development.

I can only give you the tools to guide your baby to sleep well, you are the one who needs to apply them. Sadly, there is not a magic wand for it. I would also like you to know that every baby is different, and every family is different. Some parents would say that they'd had a full night's sleep if the baby slept 3 hours straight, some if the baby slept 5 hours, but some parents will only say that the baby slept through the night if they had 10 hours of sleep. Don't compare yourself, your baby, and your family, to others.

You are not alone in this journey. Many parents are going through the same struggles. Take time, follow your intuition, and progress will follow. Your baby might not be ready today but might be ready in 7 days. So, please don't underestimate your baby's ability to learn, and keep trying. Have faith in yourself and your lovely little bundle of joy!

Common Sleep Myths

Sleep Like a Baby

This one I have already mentioned above but let's dive a bit more into it shall we?
Babies are extremely noisy sleepers, do not worry, it is normal; they might squirm and cry - but not fully cry - because their digestive system is processing the milk, or they are releasing trapped wind, or need to burp. Babies have tiny airways, and their breathing is louder. Also their sleep cycles are rocky.

Sleep When Baby Sleeps

Quite often, we hear this line: sleep when the baby sleeps, and maybe this worked like magic when the whole village was raising the baby. But since that time, lots of things have changed. Many mothers struggle with this, and there is a good reason for it. Often, we live in big cities and no longer have support from the village. Societal changes, such as urbanisation and the breakdown of traditional community structures, have led to this lack of support for new mothers. In the past, mothers needed to rest for the first forty days after the baby is born. In most cultures around the world, that is still the case.

Newborn Mothers were at home, bonding and resting with their babies, while the whole village managed the household and kept it running smoothly. Once upon a time, a village was the most natural environment where children could grow up. The village would be a community where everyone knew each other; they would share joy and hard times and nurture and help each other.

Without that village and support system from a child's birth, mothers today are feeling incredible guilt I am sure that every mother reading this will at one point have felt guilty about something. So how should she sleep when the baby sleeps? Things must be done.

Clients that I worked with are all feeling some sort of mother's guilt. Mothers now days have more freedom, but it comes with a heavy burden because they feel they need to do more. There is a pressure from society, which often sets unrealistic standards for mothers.

Mothers now days have to work, run a home, look after baby and other children, they have to look great, be independent.

Babies Shouldn't Cry

Through our adult lives society is telling us not to cry,

but if you look into science, crying is healthy. As adults, we cry due to sadness, joy, stress and empathy. In my experience, after crying, I have always felt so much better.

Crying serves its purpose for both adults and babies. It is biological and normal. Crying restores emotional balance and strengthens individual bonds, including the special bond between you and your baby.

Babies cry from the moment they are born. For babies, crying means communication; your baby can't talk, so the baby will communicate with you by crying, signalling for you to respond to their needs.

In my experience, most of the families I have been working with didn't like baby crying; some of the parents panicked, especially some of the dads. They couldn't cope with crying babies. I understand that you, as a parent, don’t like seeing your baby cry, or it makes you feel uncomfortable.

But what if I tell you this is the only way your baby communicates with you? They express their emotions by crying, like sadness, discomfort, hunger, and pain. These emotions are normal, just like happy ones.

Crying helps to self-soothe and relieves pain, some babies cry before they fall asleep, they are self-soothing. Crying relieves stress and can help us sleep better. Crying can improve mood and create emotional balance; in both you and baby.

Next time your baby is crying, remember that your baby is talking to you, they’re getting your attention, making sure that their needs are met. By responding to them, you are meeting their needs at that present moment. They might continue crying, but you have done all you could. You have responded, and now you are helping your baby to deal with their emotions, you are teaching them it is ok to cry, you are giving them a skill for life.

Studies from 2011 showed that resisting the urge to cry, lowered immune response and could affect mental health and lead to anxiety and depression in adults

Dream Feeds Don't Work

Dream feed is another subject that is very important to address. I am a fan and believe it works and I would suggest a dream feed, but not in every case. I like the fact that dream feed works wonders for sleep-deprived mums.

There are lots of experts who don't believe in dream feed or have mixed feelings about it. They say that dream feed doesn't help your baby get more sleep, (I agree), but it will shift one of the feeds a little bit later. And I also agree with this fact.

Some of the experts are saying that by dream feeding you are interrupting your baby's natural rhythms and feeding them when not hungry. Dream feeding is initiated by parents not babies.

From my experience a dream feed has helped so many Mums, and looking back I don't regret suggesting it, as they have gained an extra few hours of sleep and felt amazing the next day.

In my 25 years of experience, I haven't encountered one Mummy who wasn't happy with me suggesting a dream feed. They loved it. They could get a longer stretch of sleep. They could do a dream feed around their schedule and timing that worked for them. Dream feeding gives mums hope, they feel empowered and greatly relieved by sleeping longer.

Let's start with the definition of dream feeding: what is it, and does it work? Dream feeding, when done correctly and with the right guidance, can be a safe and effective method to help your baby sleep longer stretches.

Dream feeding is just as its name suggests; it involves feeding your baby while they are drowsy, not fully awake. It happens later in the night, just before you go to bed, between 10 and 11pm, usually 2 to 3 hours after you have put your baby down. When you are dream-feeding, you are semi-waking your baby and feeding them.

When a dream feed is incorporated into your baby's routine, you may notice an improvement in their sleep patterns and feeding habits. This can be a source of great satisfaction and a sense of accomplishment for parents.

Dream feeding is also beneficial in some cases, for example if you would like to increase your milk supply or when your baby has difficulties putting the weight on. That one extra feed could make a difference.

"Keeping your baby awake for long periods of time will mean they will sleep better..."

Babies that I have worked with that ate and slept well during the day, quite often have better nights than ones who didn't. Full feeds and regular naps, during the day will reflect on your night, there is a chance that baby will sleep better, giving you sense of relief and a good night sleep.

It's crucial to understand that keeping your baby awake for extended periods can lead to overtiredness. Newborns have sleep pressure, a key factor in their sleep patterns, and pushing them to stay awake longer in the hope of better sleep, is a risky strategy. Understanding this can empower you as a parent.

If you miss that sleep window opportunity, your baby will not only be stressed out, overtired, and overwhelmed, but they will also cry more and need you more to regulate their emotions. They won't be easy to soothe. At the same time, it will be much more difficult for you to put that baby to sleep.

Babies need their sleep. Don't try to keep them awake for long periods of time; let them sleep when they are tired. Sleep promotes sleep.

**“When a baby is born,
so is a mother.”**

Julia Jones

Chapter 4

Understanding Newborns

This chapter is packed with crucial information. You might question its relevance to sleep, but I assure you, every detail is essential. This knowledge will form the stepping stones for you to the stages that follow. Trust me, it will all fall into place.

Sleep Shaping

Sleep shaping is the process that will create positive sleep associations while gently guiding your newborn towards a consistent sleep routine.

Sleep shaping is not an overnight magic, it works gradually without adding to much stress.

Sleep shaping is ideal for babies who are 6 months and younger. It is a process that every parent can use when baby goes down for a nap or sleep.

Sleep shaping in a newborn is the first, most crucial step towards your sleeping goals. It is never too early to start. Keep it consistent, and you will find yourself focused and calm, you and your baby will gradually become more confident in what you do. Remember, confidence is built step by step.

Here are some of the sleep shaping steps:

- Begin a calming bedtime routine

- Create a sleep friendly environment
- Focus on day and night cues
- Encourage self-soothing
- Stick to age-appropriate wake window
- Try to separate feedings from sleep

More about them all in chapter 4 and 5.

Newborn Naps

At this stage naps will be all over the place, you are bonding with your baby, this is all new to you and a rigid schedule is needed on top of everything you are going through. Follow your baby's lead, feed them on demand and get to know them and all their cues. Try to give your baby a chance to nap frequently.

Here are the things you want to bear in mind.
Please don't let your baby sleep longer than 4 hours during the day. I would suggest wake them up every 3 hours for a feed. This will help your baby to maximise the number of feedings and calorie intake, and your baby will nap well which will lead to longer sleep stretches at night.
If your newborn was awake for an hour, they will need a nap. Your baby might have trouble falling asleep if you wait for longer.

Day vs. Night

Around week 2 when you have established your feedings and your baby is growing well, you will know their cues and cries. This is the time when you can begin to teach your baby the difference between day and night. Your baby won't recognise the difference between day and night just yet, but these steps might help them to link day and night more easily when they are ready.

During the Day play and interact with your baby as much as possible, when they are awake. Open the curtains when you wake up, say good morning; every day, even on the weekend. This will signal your baby it is a daytime. Expose your baby to the daylight during the day. Let them see and feel and hear the world. Let them hear all the sounds when awake but when they are asleep, keep the noise down to the minimum. Use white noise to mask the sounds around them.

During the Night dim the lights, keep noise level down and keep your energy calm and settled. Stimulation should be kept to a minimum. Keep the room as dark as possible. I like to have a Himalayan salt lamp as a night lamp, it has this amazing natural orange glow that is calming and soothing. If you don't have a salt lamp, just put a kitchen towel over your little lamp and that will dim the lights as well.

Wake Window vs Sleep Window

Wake window is the period when your baby is awake. Your baby's wake up window starts from the moment you have picked them up from their bed and until you put them down for the next nap. Wake window will also depend on the length of the previous nap.
Let me help you understand wake up windows and their importance.

Your baby has limits on how long they can stay comfortably awake. Exceeding these limits will lead to overtiredness and instead of calming melatonin, your baby will be having a rush of cortisol, making it harder for them to fall asleep and stay asleep.

Your overtired baby will also be more likely to get into a cycle of bad naps and poor night sleep.
Sleep window is the optimal period when a baby can fall asleep easily. It is the perfect time when their brain as well as their body, are naturally ready for sleep. When you are in tune with your baby's sleep window, falling asleep will be smoother and easier and will give your baby better sleep quality for longer.

Wake Window by Age

Age	Wake window	Naps
0-4 weeks	45 min, max 60min	Multiple naps
1 month	60 min	Multiple naps
2 months	60-75 min	4 naps
3 months	75-90 min	4 naps
4 months	1.5 - 2 hours	4 naps
5 - 6 months	2 - 2.5 hours	3 naps
7 - 11 months	2.5 - 3.5 hours	2 naps
12 -14 months	4.5 - 5 hours	1 nap

Cat Naps

A cat nap is basically a short nap, it lasts between 20 to 45 minutes, sometimes less. Catnapping is when your baby sleeps only one sleep cycle at the time, they are not able to re-settle or connect these sleep cycles and therefore they can't go into deep, restorative sleep.

There are a few things that could cause baby's cat naps:

- Baby wake window was too short, your baby won't be able to fall asleep or may fall asleep but won't stay asleep.
- Developmental changes
- Illness
- Hunger

Most babies will start to cat nap between age 6-8 weeks. Around week 8 your baby's maternal melatonin is wearing off, so that is the stage when they might appear harder to settle.

Baby Cues and Crying

Recognising Baby Cues

What are baby cues? Baby cues are sets of movements, sounds, and facial expressions used by your baby to communicate with you before they develop words. Cues are the ways your baby shows you how they feel. When you learn how to read these cues you will know what their feelings and needs are. Your baby is constantly communicating with you. Pay attention.

Those first precious weeks are all about getting to know your baby. That is why the first weeks of your baby's life are so important to focus only on you two.

If you pay attention to your baby's cues, you will be able to interpret them. Some of them are very similar.

Here are some examples:

- The baby who is tired will try to tell you **I am sleepy** by rubbing their eyes, pulling their ears and not having eye contact, instead staring into the distance.

- If your baby for instance gets red in their face, kicks and raises their legs while breathing a bit faster, they are saying **I need a burp** or **I need a change of activity.**

- When your baby is looking for kind of excited, looking like they might clap and waving their hands and you see their mouth shape like they are trying to say 'ooaa' with their eyes wide open, they are telling you. **I want to play.**

- **I am hungry** is the most obvious one. Hungry babies are looking for a source of food with their mouths. They might look like they want to latch onto your fingers, noses, hands. This cue is called rooting, and it is a natural thing babies do when they are hungry.

If your baby is not really engaging in a play or is starting to turn their heads away from yours while you are playing, they might be saying **I've had enough**, this cue usually comes after babies getting overstimulated and can't cope anymore.

Reasons for Crying

Babies cry for different reasons and babies cry a lot. On average, your baby will cry for around 2-3 hours per day in their first months. That will be the most crying than at any other point in their lives. So, if you experience your baby crying a lot, it is normal. Just give them lots of reassurance and cuddles and love, let them know that you are there for them.

In the early stage of their life, babies don't cry because they want to, they cry because they need to. Let me explain this. If we compare human babies to the animal babies, some animal babies can walk, see and hear just hours after they are born. This is because their brains are almost completely developed. And that is exactly what makes humans unique.

Humans need a big brain. Human babies are born with largely immature brains, your newborn will have a little control over their movements. Science says that human babies are born about 12 months early. Mother nature didn't leave that to chance, there is good reason for that. Hence the reason why all babies are born with 2 soft spots on their head, one at the top and one at the back. These soft spots will allow your baby's skull to expand, giving enough room for the rapid brain growth that happens in the first 12 months of their life. If your baby was born when their brain was fully developed, the size of their head would be much bigger, and mothers' hips would have to be completely different.

Let's now go back to crying, shall we? When your baby cries, try to cuddle them, hug them. Your hugs have healing properties. It will help them relax and promote the flow of the love hormone, oxytocin, which can help balance out stress hormones.

Your baby will cry when **needing a cuddle**, when **they have had enough**, this often happens when they are overstimulated. Your baby might cry when **they are bored**. One minute they will be happy, just lying there observing or playing on their own and suddenly, they will start to cry. This is because **they need your attention**.

Your baby also might cry because **they are tired**. To prevent your baby from overtiredness, look for these tired cues. Your baby will suddenly get very quiet and still, your baby will stare into space, your baby might start rubbing and touching their eyes, their eyebrows might start becoming red. In newborns it is harder to see the cues of tiredness and sometimes you will miss them, but your baby will let you know. If you miss these cues and your baby is overtired, they will cry.

Your baby will also cry if **they are too hot or cold**. The best place to check their temperature would be on their back or tummy, then decide if you need more layers or must take a layer off. Your baby's hands and feet will often be cold, but that doesn't really mean that they are cold. Cold hands and feet in babies often happen as their circulation system is not still developed properly, blood in newborns runs to their vital organs first.

As your baby has a very small stomach, they will need frequent feeds. **Hunger** is also another reason why your baby cries. If they are smacking their lips and trying to suck your finger, nose or other parts of your body, they are rooting as I have mentioned before in

baby cues. Rooting is a reflex reaction when your baby is hungry and trying to find a source of milk.
Sometimes you will check all the cues, try everything but nothing will work. That can be exhausting. Hearing your baby cry can be a very distressing thing for parents. Some parents are more sensitive to babies crying than others. Sometimes babies will cry and cry and cry some more. Please try to understand that coming out of the womb, where they were nice and snuggled and safe, could be scary. By being born, your baby has come to a new environment, and they sometimes just cry to regulate themself.

As your newborn baby grows, they may start to cry louder and more frequently around week 2 of their life. Get ready for that. Their cry might get longer during the next few weeks and will hit the peak around 6 to 8 weeks of life.

What is Colic?

Colic in babies is frequent and can result in severe crying with fussiness and no clear cause, usually due to abdominal pain or discomfort. Colicky babies often cry more in the late afternoon and evening. Colic is very common in babies. 1 in 4 newborn babies might have it and it is most common during the first 6 weeks of life. Colic usually goes away on its own when the baby turns 3 months old.

Your baby has colic if they cry 3 hours a day for 3 or more days a week over 3 weeks. If your baby is colicky, they will be very fussy, gassy, and won't sleep well.
Colicky babies will often pass lots of gas or will be burping a lot. Usually that relates to them swallowing lots of air while crying. Colicky babies will have a bright red face and tight belly. As they have

discomfort, they will often curl up their legs and clench their fists.
If you are breastfeeding, try to avoid some foods like milk, eggs, nuts or wheat for some time.

What to do When a Baby is Crying?

Dealing with babies crying can be stressful. Especially if you have a baby who suffers from Colic.

Try to find a trusted adult, family member, or a friend and let them care for the baby from time to time. It is important for parents to take a break. Distancing yourself, even for a little while, will reduce your stress level and might help your baby as well. Babies are very sensitive and can pick up on your energy.

There are parents who have no help, and this period is extremely challenging. But here are some things you can do to help. Try comforting the baby, chat to them, try skin to skin contact, stroke them, sing them a song, rock them, go outside for a walk, give them a warm bath, offer the dummy if needed, make sure your baby is not hungry. Try frequently to change your baby's position, sometimes a car ride will help as its motion will often soothe your baby. White noise has lots of settings, try to change them frequently, different noise might also calm a fussy baby. Keep any stimulation to a minimum.

Most of the parents that had colicky baby said it was the most challenging period of their baby's life.

"Sleep,
eat,
play,
repeat
..."

Luiza DeSouza

Chapter 5

Comfort and Feeding

Sleep and Feeding Connection

Focus on Feedings

When you bring your baby home from the hospital, it could be a bit overwhelming and not only for your baby who has just realised they are no longer in the womb, but for you as a parent as well. Many parents are not aware how exhausting parenthood is in the early days, in the first few months.

In the early days I would suggest you focus primarily on feeding and bonding. When I talk about forming positive sleep habits, with newborns, feeding is my go-to. There is a strong connection between feeding and sleep. As we all know, a hungry baby will not sleep well. At the newborn stage please don't worry about baby sleep patterns, they will fall naturally into place, if feeding is good. Please make sure that every feed counts; if your baby has a nice full tummy after each feed, they are more likely to have a good long nap.

If you choose to breastfeed, while you are frequently feeding your baby, you will establish a good milk supply. I strongly believe that if the baby feeds well and has a great intake of calories during the day that will reflect on their sleep when night comes. If you choose to bottle feed, it will be a bit easier in a sense, as you will know how much milk the baby has taken.

Breastfeeding or Bottle Feeding?

This is very sensitive subject. I believe that every mother should be able to decide either to breastfeed or bottle feed. I support both. There is no right or wrong way of feeding your baby. I understand that breastfeeding is pushed upon us for the right reasons. And I am sure that every mother's first choice would be breastfeeding at least for the first few months. But Some of the mothers struggle to breastfeed. And sadly, breastfeeding is not an option for them for various reasons.

If you are one of these mothers who struggle with breastfeeding, I feel for you. I have seen how these mothers are affected, as guilt and shame washes over them. They suffer silently. The thoughts of not being good enough are always at the back of their mind. They feel like they are failing as mothers, when unable to breastfeed. I strongly believe that there should be equal support for mothers who bottle feed. Parenthood is very polarised these days. Breastfed or bottle fed, baby will grow; what it comes down to is that all parents want the best for their child

Active and Responsive Feeding

Breastfeeding

First thing to do when breastfeeding is to make sure that your baby is un-swaddled and fully awake. If your baby falls asleep while they are feeding, which is often a case in newborns, wake them up by tickling their toes, changing their nappy, and taking their clothes off, turn the lights on; you want to bother them just enough to keep them awake for long enough for that full active feed.

Active feeding is important to establish good feeding patterns. When your baby has an active feed and a full tummy, they will settle easier to sleep on their own in a moses basket or crib.

Good latch means better feed and equals high milk flow. You can tell your baby's latch is good by watching the jaw movement. If the jaw movement is happening all the way back to the ear, that is a sign of active feed. With good latch, you will be able to hear swallowing, and the baby will from time to time, take a small rest.

On the other hand, if the chin is going up and down and lips are moving, that is called butterfly sucking. When baby is only suckling, active feeding has stopped; the baby is not actively feeding any more. Poor latch will result in low milk flow and can damage your nipples and cause discomfort and pain.

Bottle Feeding

When bottle feeding your baby try to keep the bottle in a horizontal position to prevent milk from flowing too fast. When bottle feeding, I would suggest taking a short break after every ounce to burp your baby.

Burping or winding is an important part of feeding. While your baby is feeding, they can swallow air bubbles that can cause a lot of discomfort if trapped in the tummy. Burp your baby well, during and after a feed.

How do You Know if Your Baby Had a Full Feed?

If your baby is breastfeeding it is hard to tell as you can't measure how much your baby drank. Here is a little tip. Have you ever noticed your baby has tight fists, when you start the feed, but once your baby is full, they relax? If you think your baby has had enough milk, lift their arm, if their arm falls back down, this is most likely a sign that they had a full feed. If you put the baby's arm up and they pull it back, your baby might be still hungry.

Responsive Feeding

Responsive feeding or feeding on demand is simply feeding your baby when they signal that they are hungry. This is an important part of establishing your milk supply if breastfeeding while you are bonding with your baby. Also, in those early days your baby has a tiny tummy so frequent feedings will have to be in place.

Let me lead you through your baby's stomach capacity: This will be handy for bottle-fed babies as with breastfeeding it is hard to tell how much milk your baby has had.

On day one your baby's stomach is the size of a cherry, and they will need small frequent feeds 5-7ml. On day 3 your milk production will increase, and this will encourage your baby to feed more frequently. Now the baby's stomach is the size of a walnut, and they will take 22-27 ml per feed.

When your baby is one week old and their stomach is the size of the apricot, they will take 45-60 ml per feed.

When your baby has reached their first month milestone and their frequent feedings have helped establish the milk supply, your baby will now drink 80-150 ml per feed as their stomach is now the size of the egg.

Once you and your baby have established good breastfeeding, space out the feeds gradually and make sure that every feed is a full, focused and good feed. As your baby grows, you will witness bigger feeds, spaced out, every 3 hours. That will increase calorie intake during the day.

Bottle fed babies will need to feed about every 3 to 4 hours.

Responsive feeding is great to start with, but if you let your baby constantly "snack feed" instead of giving them a full feed, it is less likely that your baby will be full enough to keep them going through the naps. Instead, they will end up waking frequently.

When Not to Feed

Babies shouldn't be fed every time they cry.

Writing this will raise lots of eyebrows and not many mothers will agree with me. But hear me out. We live in a world were emotional eating leads to obesity. I want you to be aware that every time your baby cries doesn't mean they are hungry. Quite often I see mothers offering their baby a breast or a bottle to stop their baby from crying. If you feed your baby every time they cry, your baby might grow up feeling that food is the answer to every emotional need.

Feeding them every time they cry might also lead to snack feeding which leads to more frequent waking out of hunger.

I understand it is hard to hear your little one cry, but instead of giving them a bottle or a breast, straight away, please stop and listen as the baby cries for reasons other than hunger; all this is explained above in **why babies cry**. Make sure you figure out the right reason and then act accordingly.

Sleep, Eat, Wake Cycle

When your baby wakes up from their nap, the first thing you should do is to feed them 5-10 min after they wake up. If your baby is fully awake it is more likely that they will have a full active feed. After feed, it is time to play. Playtime will stimulate your baby and that is important as you want to build that sleep pressure during their wake window. Wake windows will vary in length, it depends on your baby's age, you will find specific guidance on wake windows throughout the book. While playing with your baby, at some point you will notice they are getting tired, now it is time to put them down for nap, without feeding. Repeat this eat, wake, sleep cycle, after every nap.

This eat, play, sleep schedule is a wonderfool tool, your baby will start understanding the difference between hunger and sleep. Hungry and sleep cues are similar, making it difficult. With this schedule, you will know exactly what is happening.

This can help you to free yourself from a feeding to sleep relationship. As baby learns this, it is more likely that they will fall asleep without needing your help.

Safe Sleep

Your newborn will sleep a lot during their first year of life. That is why you should follow safe sleep advice. Safe sleeping guidelines can significantly reduce the chance of Sudden Infant Death Syndrome (SIDS).

SIDS is also known as cot death. No-one knows what causes SIDS but research has shown that following safer sleep advice significantly reduces the chance of SIDS occurring.

I am following guidelines from lullaby trust. The Lullaby Trust raises awareness of SIDS and provides expert advice on safer sleep for babies.

This is what they recommend:

- Always lie your baby on their back, keep the sleep space clear and use a firm flat mattress with waterproof cover
- Sheets should be firmly tucked in
- Make sure that baby's head is not covered by swaddle or sleeping bag
- Room temperature should be between 16-20'C
- Keep your baby in smoke free environment
- Avoid your baby from overheating
- For first six months sleep in the same room as your baby, baby should sleep in a separate cot or Moses basket
- Breastfeeding lowers the risk of SIDS, I would recommend breastfeeding, but only, if possible, of course

Some research shows that dummies might also protect babies against SIDS, but that keeps on changing through the years.

For more information about safe sleep please check www.lullabytrust.org.uk

Swaddling

Swaddling is a very old tradition, where you wrap your baby in a light breathable blanket or nowadays parents often use dream pods, swaddles or swaddle bags.

Newborns have a startle reflex that can wake them up. Startle reflex or the Moro reflex is normal, and all healthy babies have it for the first few months of their life. Startle reflex can wake up your baby. Swaddling will limit that movement. Not only that, the pressure of swaddling mimics the feeling of the womb and most of the newborns are happy when swaddled, in my experience, they sleep for longer.

When swaddling your baby, make sure you reduce the layers of clothing, so your baby doesn't overheat and please don't cover your baby's face or ears. One more thing to keep in mind when swaddling newborn, their upper body can be swaddle tightly, but leave their legs looser, for hip mobility.

Some babies might not want to be swaddled and that is ok. You don't need to force it. If your baby loves swaddling, stop it somewhere between 4 and 6 months and move to sleeping bag.

Skin to Skin Contact

Once your baby is born, they have to get used to all their new surroundings, offering skin to skin contact will help your baby adjust to their environment. Skin to skin contact is not only encouraging emotional bonding but will also increase your milk supply and will stimulate your baby's feeding instincts, whether baby is breast or bottle feed. Skin to skin reduces postnatal recovery.

You should lay a naked baby (with nappy on) on your bare chest. This way the baby can hear the comforting sounds of your heartbeat. Skin to skin contact will also regulate the baby's heart rate as well as breathing and temperature.

Dummies

In all honesty I don't mind dummies, there is so much to be said about them in the early months of your child's life. They are magical tools that work wonders and will help you immensely for calming your baby. If you choose to go on the dummy path here are a few things I would like to point out.

Sucking is the first and most natural instinct for babies, this way they soothe easily. Babies have an urge to suck especially in the first few weeks. But if you are breastfeeding, use of a dummy is not advisable until your breastfeeding is well established, and a dummy shouldn't be introduced before 4 weeks of age. This will also help your baby avoid "nipple confusion".

"Nipple confusion" is when your baby has difficulty latching onto the breast during early introduction of a dummy or a teat. The reason why this is happening is that your baby is using different sucking techniques.

I would also like to point out that Lullaby trust guidelines suggest that in some research using a dummy when you put your baby to sleep might reduce the risk of SIDS.

Dummies can also be beneficial if you have a colicky baby. They provide instant relaxation and will prevent your baby from further crying. Sucking on dummy will trigger relaxation and can help with gas moving through your baby's gut; dummies will also limit intake of air. If you have a colicky baby, a dummy will be a big help to you as a parent and your crying baby.

Here are some downsides that I have seen in my work connected with the use of a dummy. Once your baby has a sleep association with a dummy, it is hard to get rid of them. Also, around months 4 of age, quite often they will spit the dummy out, but because they can't put it back in without your help, they will cry. This can happen repeatedly at night. So, before you choose one, it is something to be aware of.

If your baby is very gassy, dummies can make this even trickier because, when they suck on a dummy, they tend to swallow more air.

Bathtime

Your newborn doesn't need to be bathed every day. For the first 2 months, give them a bath every second day and use only water, so that their gentle skin doesn't get dry. For the first 2-3 weeks, I would only use a flannel bath, to wipe your baby clean using warm water and a flannel.

Experience of the first bath is very exciting. It is a special time for you and your baby to bond. At the first bath I would highly suggest for you to have an extra pair of hands, it would be great if you and your partner or husband can experience it together. Create a calming atmosphere, dim the lights and let gentle music in the background.

I wouldn't recommend giving your baby a proper bath until the umbilical cord falls off. Around week 2 or 3. You want to keep the area around the umbilical cord dry. By week 3 you will also feel much more comfortable and in tune with your baby, once the umbilical cord falls off whole process of bathing will get easier.

I have not come across a baby who doesn't love their bath. The only reason why babies cry when bathed is because the water is too cold. Ideal temperature for a baby's bath is between 37'c and 38'c. Bath time with a newborn should only be 5 minutes.

Never start a bath if your baby is hungry, tired or getting near feed. You want your baby to be in good spirits when taking a bath. If your baby is a bit fussy in the bath, why don't you try a swaddle bath? You can learn how to swaddle bath below.

Swaddle Bathing

If your baby is a bit fussy it could be that the baby's temperature is dropping, and your baby is cold. A swaddle bath can really help with this. A swaddle bath is suitable for premature and very young babies and allows them to feel like they are in a little cocoon, the way they have felt in your womb.

How to swaddle in the bath? Loosely wrap your baby in a small muslin and submerge them into the bath. Swaddle bathing will decrease temperature loss, will stabilise energy levels, and mean that your baby is less likely to cry.

Neck and Head

When baby is born, they will have no control of their head as their neck muscles have not fully developed yet. Compared to their body, baby's head is big therefore you will need to support their head while holding them until they develop neck strength and can hold their heads up. That will come around 3 months of age.

It's perfectly normal for newborns to have a preferred side to turn their heads onto. This is a natural part of their development, but it can lead to tightening of the neck muscles, making it harder for them to turn their heads in opposite directions. This can cause flat heads in babies or make breastfeeding challenging.

To lessen the chance of developing these conditions, make sure they turn their heads frequently. This might be challenging in the first eight weeks of life, so you need to help them. It would be great if you could swap their sides, gently moving their heads from one side to the other. For instance, when they are taking their first nap on their left side, try to make sure that their second nap is on the right.

Head-turning practices are essential as they build neck muscles and ensure that pressure on your baby's scalp is evenly distributed.

Tummy Time

Tummy time is essential for developing baby's head and neck muscle strength. However, it is easier said than done. Tummy time can be challenging for your baby, they might dislike it if you introduce it incorrectly.

Most babies get upset when it's tummy time to start with; with consistency and patience, your baby will grow to like it. Start with a few seconds and build it slowly up. Parents often give in because they dread that time, but when your baby is practicing every day, you will see the progress and you will be happy that you haven't give up.

There are some gentle ways of introducing tummy time, just remember to start them early, make it fun and try to do it every wake window during the day.

Every baby enjoys skin to skin time, which is great way of gently introducing tummy time. Your baby is placed on their tummy, on your chest with nappy on. How wonderful, your baby is so happy to be so close to you while practicing tummy time without knowing.

Fun tummy time on the balance ball can make any tummy time into fun activity. Your baby is placed on their tummy on a balance ball, and you rock your baby gently back and forth.

If your baby really doesn't like tummy time, try to introduce a football hold. This will ease baby and get them used to being on their tummy. Hold your baby face down, one hand should be between their legs supporting their tummy and the other should be supporting their head and neck. This position is very good for gassy babies.

This tummy time is classic. Place your baby on the ground and put a rolled-up towel or a blanket under the armpits. This will help your baby to lift their head. When you notice progress and your baby is getting stronger, remove the towel.

There are many ways you can practice tummy time with your little one I have only mentioned my favourite ones.

"Without enough sleep, we all become tall two year olds."

Jojo Jensen

Chapter 6

Welcoming Your Newborn

Congratulations on bringing your first child into this world! You have officially become a parent. This is the time when all sorts of emotion will wash over you. It is a time filled with joy, lots of changes and sometimes a bit of uncertainty. But don't you worry. You will adapt, there is no rush, you are not here to compete. Give yourself and your baby time. This is the period when you will be recovering from birth, resting and getting to know your baby.

Embrace Routine and Find Your Rhythm

If you asked me to give you only one tip, a tip that will change your and your baby's lives for the better, I would say have a routine in place. Everyone is talking about routine and there is a reason behind it. Routine offers your baby a sense of security, supports your baby's body clock and gives them emotional stability.

Babies love routine. Babies who follow routine are happier, and so are the parents. It gives both baby and parent a sense of security, as they both know what follows. Having a routine in place will build your confidence as a parent. Routine will give you an outline for the day. With a simple outline, your family will be able to go through the tasks that the day brings with ease.

It is never too early to start with routine. But in the first few weeks of your baby's life let's keep it easy and simple. Let's focus on feedings and bonding. Let's focus on your milk supply and then let's start implementing small changes that will make a big difference.

During this period, I would like to say, anything goes. Your newborn can't connect sleep cycles yet so they will need a lot of cuddles, reassurance, comfort and help to settle.

When settled, please make sure to put them down in their own sleep space, either a cot or Moses basket. Guide them, teach them and give them the opportunity to sleep independently from day one; by doing so you are giving them a chance to grow into little, independent, happy sleepers.

What to Expect

In the first few weeks, your baby will sleep a lot. Newborns are sleepy and will sleep most of the time, around 16+ hours a day. As your baby grows. this will decrease, by the time they are 3 months old, they will be sleeping 12 to 16 hours a day. At this stage you will notice that their naps are 2-3 hours long due to the need for frequent feeding.

There are a few reasons your newborn might wake up. Hunger is the first and mostly, the main reason. If they are hungry, you will know.

They might wake up when uncomfortable. If they are too hot or too cold or need a nappy change. Other times, they might have been woken up by sudden movement or a loud noise or they are no longer tired.

For now, you don't have to worry about a set schedule. Your newborn naps will be irregular. Aim for a 45-minute waking window but try to ensure that your baby is not awake for longer than an hour. Even an extra 5 minutes, can make them overtired, which can make it harder to settle them and more difficult for them to fall asleep.

At this stage, your baby's sleep will be largely dictated by the feeding schedule. As they grow, feeding patterns will change, and so will sleep. Understanding this connection will help you manage your expectations and allow you to gently structure your day.

These early days focus on feeding, caring for yourself, healing, building a bond by cuddling them, loving them, having lots of skin-to-skin contact, and simply taking their lead. Your milk supply in the early days will grow on demand. Milk is produced on demand and supply.

Every baby is different, and they all have their own rhythm. By observing and listening to their cues, you'll learn to understand their needs and respond accordingly. Following your baby's lead and trusting your instinct will empower you and build your confidence as a parent. Enjoy this journey, you are doing great, and as days pass by, you are getting to know your baby more.

Key Developments in the First 3 Months

After 9 months in your womb, the baby will enter the world, the world that they know nothing about. Everythingis new and unfamiliar, during these first months, they will go through significant physical and emotional growth. In the first 3 months, your baby will go through rapid developmental changes. They will learn to recognise sounds; they will learn how to communicate with you through their expressions and cries.

At birth, newborns are all curled up, just as they were positioned in the womb. But you will witness a transformation as your baby grows and adjusts to the outside world. They will soon begin to stretch and strengthen their muscles. One of the earliest milestones is improved neck control. Very quickly you will notice your baby lifting their head during tummy time. Tummy time is important for every baby to build a strength. Start with tummy time from day one, make it short and as they build up strength and become more comfortable, gradually increase tummy time. (more about tummy time on page 65)

This is a period when your baby is not only growing physically, but their senses are also developing. Your baby can recognise your scent from birth, and they will be able to recognise your voice. Newborns can recognise voices and are often comforted by them, research shows. Every time you speak and sing to your baby, it can be soothing. While newborn vision is limited, that will also improve as they grow. Your baby will be able to focus on objects and track moving objects around 2 months of age. Talk to them closely, they love your face.

Believe it or not, communication is also developing during these early stages. Your baby will mainly communicate with you through crying but with time, you will be able to recognise different cries (more about cues page 46). Coos and smiles will develop around 2 months, and this is start of deeper understanding and bonding with your baby.

Weeks 1-2

Feeding and Nutrition

Just after birth, during the first few days, you might notice that your baby has lost a little bit of weight. This is completely normal, nothing to worry about; this happens due to fluid loss just after birth. By the second week, your baby will want to feed a lot and will regain their weight. You will have the feeling that you are feeding constantly. A growth sprout is on the horizon, this is the time when your baby's body needs extra milk to grow Breastfeeding is nourishing your baby but is also a big energy demand for you, it can burn up to 700 calories a day if you are exclusively breast feeding. Please make sure you eat well and hydrate to keep up your energy.

Formula fed babies will eat every 3-4 hours, about 2-3 oz each feed. Whatever type of feeding you are going for, skin to skin contact is important during the first weeks of your baby's life, especially if you are nursing. Skin to skin will boost your milk supply, builds a beautiful bond between your little one and you, and will also help regulate your baby's temperature and heartbeat.

Sleep and Wake Cycles

As I mentioned, your newborn will sleep a lot, but a circadian rhythm like yours does not regulate sleep yet. Newborn sleep is guided by 'sleep pressure'.

'Sleep pressure' is a biological process that builds up during wakefulness and fades during sleep, having impact on timing and duration of sleep. Simply put, the longer your baby stays awake, the more pressure builds up, making them more likely to fall asleep.

Understanding this, can help you understand your baby's sleep needs. Always follow the waking windows charts that you'll find throughout the chapters.

Because their circadian rhythm has not developed yet, around week 2, start exposing your baby to natural light. Open the curtains, let morning light in. By making daytime active, you are encouraging daytime alertness. In the evening, create a calming, quiet environment using soft lights to signal that it is time to wind down. This introduction to day and night, will help your baby adjust easily into regular sleep patterns, and these will develop over time.

Always put your baby down to sleep on their back, on a flat surface in their crib. Make sure that the crib is empty to reduce the risk of SIDS. For more detailed information on safe sleeping practices refer to page 59.

Swaddle your baby before putting them down to sleep.

Development and Bonding

Your baby has started to communicate with you by crying. Crying is now only way they can express their needs. If they are hungry, uncomfortable, or just need a cuddle they will let you know. This is the period you might find challenging as they cry the most, but it is also normal sign of growth. By responding to their needs, you are building trust and connection with your baby.

When baby is 2 weeks old, start introducing more frequent tummy time sessions. Tummy time strengthens their neck and shoulder muscles and prevents flat spots on their head. Tummy time helps them develop gross motor skills like rolling, sitting and crawling. Your baby might not like tummy time at first, but with consistency, your baby will adjust and starting to enjoy this time more.

When your baby's umbilical cord falls off, usually between weeks 2 and 3, they will be ready for their first bath. Bathing should be a wonderful experience for you and your baby.

In 25 years of working with children, I have not encountered a baby who doesn't love their bath. The only reason babies cry is because the water is too cold. Or their body temperature drops, and therefore, they feel cold.

To make bathtime enjoyable, keep the water warm. A warm bath will signal to your baby that it is time to relax. The ideal temperature is between 37'C and 38'C.

If your baby seems unhappy and fussy add extra security and warmth by introducing a 'swaddle bath'. (All about swaddle bath on page 64)

Out and About

If you haven't been out with your baby yet, if you feel ready, start taking baby out for a bit of a fresh air. Walks can be part of your daily routine and a lovely way to share outdoor time with your new family; an especially nice routine for the weekend.

Goals for week 2
Remember practice makes it perfect

- Start practising tummy time
- Start exposing your baby to daylight first thing in the morning
- Start the bath if the umbilical cord has fallen off
- Wake window 45 min no longer than 1 hour

Week 3

Feeding and Nutrition

As your baby enters week 3, their growth spurt from week 2 continues. You'll notice your baby becoming rounder, they are filling out with adorable chubby cheeks. The growth spurt continues in week 3 as well as the focus is on feeding. Continue feeding your baby on demand, make sure they are fully fed, rather than just using you for comfort sucking.

The more calories taken in during the day, the likelier they are to sleep longer stretches at night.

For bottle fed babies make sure you are increasing the amount to 3-4 oz, every 3-4 hours.

Sleep and Wake Patterns

As you are approaching week 3 you might notice that your baby is getting more alert during the day; a bit more awake. When awake, follow a pattern of feeding, playing and when they show tired cues, settling them back to sleep. Wake window is about 45 - 60 minutes at this age.

Approaching 3 weeks your baby is still very young and could be upset when putting them down in a cot or a mosses basket for a sleep. This is normal. I will share a helpful technique, called the 'soothing ladder'. This technique supports your baby in settling down and you can start using it from week 3.

Development and Bonding

This week your baby is making exciting developmental leaps. Your baby can now turn their head to you when hearing your voice. Your baby's vision is still blurry, if you are close enough, your baby will be able to see your face, they love your face.

This is the week when baby cues are becoming noticeably distinct. Especially when they are hungry. Recognising these cues will make your feeding easier and you will be able to respond to hunger before they become too upset.

Tummy time is also becoming more enjoyable, you will notice that they can lift their head slightly now.

During week 3 your baby is crying more frequently, it is very normal for this age. Some of the babies might start showing signs of colic. (more about colic on page 50)

The colic phase can be an extremely tough phase. Stay close and offer your baby comfort and keep them secure while showering with love. You are giving them all they need; you are helping them feel safe in this new world.

The Soothing Ladder

My Go-to Technique From Week 3

'The 'Soothing Ladder' is a gentle method I came across years ago. I had been working with a baby who cried a lot, she just couldn't settle, unless she was in the buggy, on the go. I started to have doubts if I will ever be able to settle her. One week later, I came across a technique that I had never heard of before - 'The Soothing Ladder'.

Monday came, and I tested it on little one. At first, it was confusing for me and the baby, but I didn't give up, we practiced, and soon enough, I memorised all 7 steps in the right order. This whole process was uplifting. For the first time I hadn't rushed through, desperately trying to make sure that the baby didn't cry. For the first time I paused and listened. This pause made me calmer and gave baby a chance and time to settle. After only three nights, the baby could settle herself. She resonated with the technique and responded well. After day 3, I only had to go up to step 4. From that day on, this has been my go-to technique.

Quite often when baby is tired and upset, we just want to settle them as quickly as we can. That was me in this case. But me rushing, to settle her made her unsettled, the Soothing Ladder technique taught me to pause and give baby a chance to settle.

What's truly remarkable about the Soothing Ladder is its effectiveness, and the feedback that I get from parents who have tried it. By day three, every baby I've used it on has shown improvements. Consider that I have years of practice. You might need a bit more time to get used to it. You might think it is not working for you but, with practice, you will be on the right track to have a happy little independent sleeper.

The Soothing Ladder method is a gentle method developed by Heather Turgeon and Julie Wright. It gives parents a sense of calmness and guides them to respond to their baby's needs while promoting and practising the ability for their baby to fall asleep independently.

The Soothing Ladder has seven different steps. It is easy to remember, and every parent can apply it to gradually calm their baby. Start with step one, then move to a more comforting step if needed.

The Soothing Ladder gives your baby a sense of security and attachment.

This method gives your baby a chance to learn how to soothe themselves; you are giving them a chance and encouraging them to settle by not jumping in immediately.

How Does The Soothing Ladder Work?

I suggest you start this technique with the first nap of the day. The first nap of the day is always the easiest. Your baby is more likely to cruise through this when most tired. Continue to apply this method during each nap time during the day, bedtime, and after every waking during the night. The Soothing Ladder has 7 steps, you always start with step 1.

First, put your baby down drowsy but awake, and leave the room. Now wait. Your baby might fall asleep on their own. That is wonderful. But if they don't and they start crying, you start with step one. (Enter the room)

1.Enter the room

Your baby is crying. You have entered the room. Come close to the cot and give your baby time to realise that you are there. They will notice as they can smell you. Don't talk, pat, or touch your baby; just be there. Wait for 15 to 30 seconds. If the baby is still crying, move to step 2.

2. Use your voice

Your baby is crying. Now start shushing sound, start just gentle and calm. Use a shushing sound, no patting or touching. Pause for 15 to 30 seconds. Baby did not calm down, move to step 3.

3. Dummy

If your baby uses a dummy, put it back in their mouth. What worked for me was taking the current dummy out
and replacing it with a new one. Wait for 15 -30 seconds. If the baby is still crying or the baby is not using the dummy, move to step 4.

4. Your touch

Now, continue shushing and use touch. Place your hand on the baby's tummy and pat gently. If your baby calms down and falls asleep, that's great. The aim of this technique is to let the baby fall asleep in the cot, not in your arms. Pause 15 – 30 seconds. If the baby still needs your support, let's move to step 5.

5. Jiggle
You will continue with shushing, but now you will jiggle your baby gently. Sometimes, just jiggling motions side to side will help your baby fall asleep. Wait for 15 -30 seconds. If the baby is not settled yet, move to step 6.

6. Pick them up
When you have gone through all five steps, and none of them has helped settle your baby, it is time to pick them up. Once the baby is calmed and settled, put them down again. If you have tried this a couple of times and it is not working, move to step 7.

7. Feed them
We have come to step 7. The reason why this is the last step is that we don't want babies to associate feeding with sleep. Feeding should be nourishment.

When start using this ladder technique, you might feel like you can't remember what comes next, I felt the same way. You and your baby are just practising, every time you use 'The Soothing Ladder' it will become easier. Sometimes, you will stop on step 3, sometimes on step 5, and sometimes on step 7. Please do not get discouraged if you don't get it straight away.

Make sure you are using 'The Soothing Ladder' during naps and at night. With older babies, if it is not feeding time, I would not use step 7, as they might again just need your presence.

This method will help you in the long run. I like to introduce the Soothing Ladder during week 3, just for you to practice all the steps. By week 6 you will know all you steps in the right order.

Soothing Ladder is great for babies under 6 months. You will find this method most effective when baby is between 6 weeks and 4 -5 months old.

For each step, give your baby 15 seconds of waiting time for ages 0 to 3 months and 30 seconds for ages 4 to 6 months.

I also found this method helpful especially when sleep regressions come into the picture; your baby will cruise through as they will know how to self-soothe quickly.

SOOTHING LADDER **Start at the bottom of the ladder and work your way up** **7. FEED** **6. PICK UP AND SOOTHE** **5. JIGGLE** **4. YOUR TOUCH** **3. REPLACE DUMMY** **2. YOUR VOICE** **1. YOUR PRESENCE**
Do each step: **10-15 seconds for 0-3 months** **15-30 seconds for 4-6 months**

Goals for week 3

- Continue practicing goals from week 2
- Start practicing 'the soothing ladder' technique, just practice
- Wake window 45 min

One Month Old

A New Milestone

Feeding and Nutrition

Your baby is already one month old, can you believe it? Don't they just grow so quickly? Together you have come so far.

Your baby will keep on growing and eating a lot. If you are breastfeeding, they might want to be feed frequently and that is normal and healthy. Breastfed babies will benefit if you start introducing a daily bottle. This not only gives you more flexibility, but also creates a special bonding time with Daddy or caregivers. I recommend introducing a daily bottle, using either expressed breast milk or formula.

If you wait too long, getting used to bottle feeding could be more challenging for your baby. Introducing a bottle early on will take away unnecessary stress and will establish both breastfeeding and bottle feeding without fuss.

Bottle-fed babies will eat a bit more, 4 oz, every 3-4 hours.

Sleeping and Wake Times

Your baby is becoming more alert. Wake window is now longer about 60 minutes. This is the perfect time to start creating positive sleep associations. Start with singing a specific song each time you put them to sleep. Over time your little one will start to understand that hearing the song means it is time for sleep.

This is also great time to start a simple bedtime routine: bath for 5 minutes, a fresh nappy, gentle massage, pyjamas, a short book, swaddle, sing them their sleep song and put your baby down, drowsy but awake. The baby's bedtime routine should only take about 20-30 minutes. Bedtime routine will give your baby time to wind down.

A daily bath at this age can also help them step into a relaxed state, making it easier to fall asleep.

Development and Bonding

At one month old, your baby is ready to be introduced to high-contrast patterns and black-and-white books. Your baby's vision is improving, and they will enjoy the patterns, as they stimulate their visual development.

During the tummy time your baby might start lifting their head. If they are still unsure during tummy time sessions, try placing a book, patterns or a baby mirror in front of them, making it fun and engaging. Your baby will start to produce sounds, it is so cute to see them trying to communicate with you with coos.

Routines and Bonding Activities

Your baby is now ready for a more structured daily routine, you can start with simple sleep, eat, play, repeat schedule. This will give you and your baby a sense of stability.

Every time you put your baby down use the Soothing Ladder method. Start with rocking or cuddling them while singing their sleep song, then put them down drowsy but awake. The song will be the signal that it is time to sleep. (More about music therapy and singing on page 155)

Once you place them down in the cot or Moses basket, say good night and leave the room. Then listen. If the baby is crying, go in and start the Soothing Ladder method.

It is wonderful to see that you and your baby are so involved. Every day brings you excitement and you and your little one are growing together. Cherish these precious moments, you are doing an amazing job!

Goals for week 4

- Introducing one bottle feed a day
- Reading Black and White books
- Start singing a bedtime song
- Start practising routine Sleep, Feed, Play, Repeat
- Start introducing bedtime routine
- Suggesting bathing your baby every night

Bedtime Routine Example

- Bath no longer than 5 minutes
- Fresh nappy
- Gentle massage
- Pyjamas
- Short book
- Swaddle
- Song
- Put baby in the cot or mosses basket drowsy but awake

Two Months Old
Discovering the World Together

Feeding and Nutrition

As your baby reaches two months, their feeding patterns will become more regular. Breastfed babies will nurse every 3-4 hours. Nursing six to ten times a day is normal. Taking 4-6 oz every four hours is essential for bottle-fed babies. Regular feedings will support their growth, and more milk intake will help them stay content for longer.

Sleeping and Wake Cycle

Between 6 and 8 weeks old, your maternity melatonin leaves your baby's body, and they start produce their own. Now is a perfect time to introduce day-night routine. So far you have been letting the natural light in by opening curtains in the morning. From now on wake up your baby at the same time each morning, this way you teach their internal clock that is time to start their day. At night don't forget to make it calm and dark, especially during the bedtime routine. This routine is a great way to introduce day and night, your baby's circadian rhythm will mature between 3-4 months.

Your baby is increasing their awareness and discovering there is more to life than just sleeping, eating and crying. Continue with regular naps and try to prevent overtiredness. Put them down drowsy but awake and use a soothing ladder if needed. Your little one's wake window is between 60 - 75 minutes. You might notice they are sleeping for longer stretches at night, up to 5 hours or more, but I wouldn't worry if they don't. Every baby's rhythm is unique. Continue with bedtime routine.

Development and Bonding

That delightful baby of yours is changing so much. They are continuing to make sounds and might give you a smile or two or even a giggle. This is the perfect opportunity for you to talk to them, to copy their coos, and make sure you give them time for them to copy you.

Your baby is now responding to familiar faces and objects. They might also respond when you call their name.

As your baby is more comfortable on their tummy, they are also naturally getting more physical. Their new trick is lifting their head and shoulders while having tummy time. Increase tummy time and continue practising it.

Playtime is no longer boring. Everything that was hidden in the cupboard is coming out, simple toys, baby gym, sensory toys, mobiles. Take everything out, get on the floor and play with your baby. If you have baby mirror they will be delighted seeing reflection. They will be delighted that another baby is smiling back at them.

All this is new to them, your baby might get overstimulated and feel this is all too much. Pay attention to their cues, they will let you know if they have had enough, by fussing a bit.

Your little baby is growing, they can now actually put their hands in their mouth, and you will notice that they might use hands and suck on them to self-soothe.

Comfort and Soothing

Babies between 6 and 8 weeks are at the peak of their crying. Babies may enter a period of fussiness. This usually

happens in the late afternoon, after their last nap. This time is often called 'witching hour'. If your baby is going through

this tough period, comfort them with extra cuddles. Babies at this age find a lots of reassurance in your touch. Holding them close can often soothe them.

Goals for 2 months old

- Continue practising goals from week 4
- Waking up your baby at the same time every morning
- Increase tummy time and keep on practising it

Three Months Old

A New Milestone

Feeding and Nutrition

You have now reached 3 months—what an achievement! If you are breastfeeding, you should nurse every 3-4 hours. You will know that your baby is drinking enough milk, by having to change four to five wet nappies a day. This fact is especially useful for breastfeeding babies.

Bottle fed babies will feed every 4 hours around 5-6 oz of milk.

I must address one thing: please don't soothe your baby by offering food. Every time your baby cries, it doesn't mean that they are hungry. I know it is the easiest way to calm your little one but try other soothing techniques. Remember the soothing ladder; feeding is the last resort.

Sleeping and Wake Cycle

At 3 months, your baby's circadian rhythm is finally developed and mature.

Now, they know the difference between day and night thanks to you guiding them and showing them the difference from day to night, since they were 2 weeks old. It will be easy for them to adapt. This is also the perfect time for you to establish consistent naps, three a day.

Your 3-month-old baby will sleep around 14 - 15 hours daily, with 5-hour stretches at night. The awake window at this age is 75 – 90 minutes.

You can now set a regular bedtime. 7.30 pm should be ideal; 30-minutes give-or-take. If your baby is awake more at night, this is a sign of a growth spurt or developmental milestone.

Development and Other Milestones

Month is often called by many parents, the 'charming month'. Your baby might come out of the colic stage and crying will be replaced by constant smiles. Your baby is now more in control of their movements and becoming aware of everything around them. They are still not mobile, but that is good. What a bliss!

Witness your little bundle of joy reaching new milestones. They will lift their head to 90 degrees, showing progress from the sometimes-stressful tummy time practice. This is a perfect position for a crawl. If your baby is ready, they might surprise you with a rollover from tummy to back. They might giggle doing so as they are as surprised as you are. Your baby can also now open and shut their hands, so they will start reaching for the objects that they like while being able to notice music in the background.

The five senses are now fully developed—what a joy. It's amazing to see how they respond to the world. Provide them with books, mirrors, blocks. Read to them, sing and dance with them. Engage in conversations by copying their sounds and letting them copy yours.

Goals for 3 months old

- Continue practising goals from previous month

“If you get tired, learn to rest, not to quit.”

Banksy

Chapter 7

Baby Sleep (4-6 Months)

Four Months Old

Developmental Progression, Sleep Regression

Feeding and Nutrition

As your baby reaches four months, feeding will be more predictable. Your four month old baby will nurse every 3 to 4 hours. If you are breastfeeding, it is hard to say how much milk your baby is getting. A great indicator for you at this age is wet nappies. 4-5 wet nappies daily mean they are getting enough milk.

Bottle fed babies will feed every 3 to 5 hours, aim for 4 – 6 oz per feeding. If you are expressing, your baby will need 25 oz spread during the day.

Sleeping and Wake Cycle

A 4-month-old baby will sleep between 13 and 16 hours a day, split into four daytime naps and longer night stretches. Naps shouldn't exceed 4 hours during the day otherwise, that will affect your nights. Two naps should be in the cot, and the other two can be on the go. I would suggest you make sure that the first and third naps of the day are in cot.

Make sure that naps are not longer than 2.5 hours. The wake window is 1.5-2 hours max. At 4 months of age, we are using wake windows to build a schedule.

You are now more confident and feeling like you are finally getting your baby to sleep longer stretches. But suddenly, out of nowhere, your baby is starting to wake up more frequently. They are very restless and hard to put down to sleep.

Then, the question arises in your head: What am I doing wrong? Nobody is making any mistakes. Your baby is going through developmental progression, which will cause a sleep regression. Sleep will, during regression, feel a bit off.

This regression is connected to sleep cycles, they are becoming more complex. Your baby's sleep cycles are now looking a bit more like ours. Sleep cycles will last 45 – 60 minutes and your baby will now go through four stages of sleep. You might notice that they are fighting sleep, please understand that your baby is getting used to new stages of sleep. It might take longer, sometimes up to 20 min, for the baby to fall asleep.

Sleep regression can last a few days to weeks. Your baby will need more support than ever. Sleep dependence is common during the regression period.

Dear Mummy, if you have implemented and practised all the goals from week 2, your baby by now has a good sleep foundation. Keep your bedtime and nap times the same as before, that familiarity will give them a sense of safety, while so many things feel unsettling for them. If you had a
good and independent sleeper before you hit the sleep

regression, you might go through this period faster. Somebabies might just cruise through this period. It might be your baby.

Ideal 4 months old sleep routine

Wake up
1.5 hours awake
Nap 1
1.5 hours awake
Nap 2
1.5 hours awake
Nap 3
1.5 hours awake
Nap 4
1.5 hours awake
Bedtime

Development and Bonding

This period is all about having fun playing with your baby. How wonderful it is that you have finally reached the point where your baby is more mobile and can show you all the skills, you have been practising together, such as rolling and pushing up. Rolling over is so much fun, please keep a close eye on them. You can't leave them on their own any more. The floor is the safest place where they can explore without restrictions. It is the perfect time to get on that floor and play.

Baby senses are rapidly developing. Your baby is able now to see colours, especially green and red. Make sure you are now taking out all those colourful books and enjoy reading together.

Continue enjoying your lovely little chats. Music and rhythm are great ways for both of you to express yourself. It can be fun and calming (music therapy on page 155)

This is the time when the fun of teething might also take place. Get ready for this. You will have them drooling constantly. Your baby might be restless and fussier than usual. Some babies will just cruise through this period, while others may struggle.

Tips for 4 months old

- Expect sleep regression, but that is due to developmental progress
- Now it is time to stick to the routine, check the schedule above

Five Months Old

Exploring, Growing and Engaging

Feeding and Nutrition

Feeding a 5-month-old baby is going to be a challenge. Babies at this age are curious and like to see what is happening around them, so if you are feeding them, try to get into a room where nothing much is happening. Keep it boring, that way baby is focused on the feed alone. As they grow, so does their appetite.

Breastfeeding babies should be fed every 3 - 4 hours. You can notice that your boobs feel kind of empty and soft at times. This is because breastfeeding changes as your baby grows. Nutrients and the amount of milk that you producewill adapt to your baby's needs.

If you are expressing, your baby will need 25 oz spread during the day. Bottle fed babies should have 5-6 oz every 4 hours.

Sleeping and Wake Cycle

Your baby has passed, or is passing sleep regression and suddenly, everything changes.

Sleeping now should be much better at night.

Your 5-month-old should have 3 naps a day. Around 3.5 hours of day sleep and 10-12 hours of night sleep. The wake-up window at this age is 2 to 2.5 hours.

Recommended bedtime for 5 months old is around 7pm. Give or take 30 min. Drowsy but awake practice is now paying off.

If you baby is struggling to fall asleep on their own, it is usually due to sleep association. If they depend on you to fall asleep, whenever they wake at night, they need you to help them to fall back to sleep.

Practice with them drowsy but awake, and use all other goals mentioned before in this book, starting from week 2.

5 to 6 months is a soft spot, the perfect time to help them self soothe if they are not doing it yet. If you are struggling remember to use a soothing ladder for up to 6 months to your advantage. Practice makes perfect, as does consistency. Remember, it will happen, be patient.

Ideal 5 Months Old Sleep Routine

Wake up
2 hours awake
Nap 1
2.5 hours awake
Nap 2
2.5 hours awake
Nap 3
2.5 hours awake
Bedtime

Developmental Milestones

Your baby is much bigger and better at doing things. Their hands and feet are now moving constantly, and they are finding different ways to play with them. They can roll over in both directions and are more comfortable and steadier in the seating position.

Your baby is now able to hold objects with both hands and can transfer objects from one hand to another.

In month 5, the baby demands more of your attention and communication. Make sure you give your baby plenty of opportunities to play and explore with you by their side.

Play with your baby and be present at least 3 times daily for 10 minutes.

This one-to-one focussed play will build the emotional bond. It is crucial for development of their nervous system.

One-to-one interaction will develop and provide the best foundation in life, with eagerness to learn, self-awareness, trust, and consideration for others.

Your baby loves tummy time and takes fun to another level. They may be trying to get into crawling position, or they are trying to crawl.

Your 5 month-old is social butterfly, loves to laugh and babble. Introduce a game of peek-a-boo. You might notice that your baby is having a favourite toy, song, activities.

While chatting to your baby use 'Mumma' and 'Dada' sounds. They will be looking at your face and mouth and will try to repeat it. What their first word is going to be?

Sample of 5 and 6 Months Old Sleep and Feeding Schedule	
Time	Activity
7.00 am	Wake up, feeding and play
9.00 am	Nap 1 (1-1.5 hours)
10.30 am	Wake up, feeding and play
12.30 am	Nap 2 (1-1.5 hours)
2.00 pm	Wake up, feeding and play
4.30 pm	Nap 3 (45 min)
5.15 pm	Wake up, gentle play and feed
6.00 pm	Bath and bedtime routine
6.30 pm	Feed
7.00 pm	Bedtime

Six Months Old

A New Stage of Exploration and Independence

You are now stepping into the 6th month of your motherhood journey. When you look back at it, it might have been challenging, but it is worth it. All those sleepless nights left some of the memories in a blur, but you made it. 6 months ago, you didn't really know what to do, but look at you now, you are a super mummy! All you needed was practice and consistency, which gave you a sense of accomplishment and also gave you confidence.

Feeding

As your baby is approaching six months, solid foods should gradually be introduced; exciting times, new textures, new food. Milk or formula are still their main sources of nutrition. Bottle-fed babies should have 6 to 8 oz around 6 times a day. If you are breastfeeding, nurse your baby every 4 hours.

Sleeping

This is such a lovely age; you now have a big baby. Everything is exciting. The waking window is now bigger, you have a chance to start proper activities and playgroups and socialise more. Your baby will show you obvious signs of tiredness.

Some people think a baby undergoes a 6-month sleep regression, but I can't entirely agree. If your baby is out of character, wants to eat more, or is cranky, it could indicate growth spurts. This is the period when your baby needs more food and will start weaning. That might slightly effect sleep and bowel movement.

Your baby is also rolling; this might wake the baby. Some of the babies will roll over in their sleep but then won't be able to roll back. They will call you to help them roll back.

When baby is awake, try to include them in your chores; they will find it fascinating.

Ideal 6 Months Old Sleep Routine

Wake up
2 hours awake
Nap 1
2.5 hours awake
Nap 2
2.5 hours awake
Nap 3
2.5 hours awake
Bedtime

Development

So, let's see what is waiting for you in month 6. Your baby gets very excited at times, flapping their hands and legs at the same time. Excitement quite often happens when you call their name or they see familiar faces or objects.

Six-month-olds can become very opinionated, they know what they want and might cry when someone new holds them. Your baby is responsive to all noises around them. They tend to turn their heads quickly and respond to sound.

Your big baby can make some sounds and copy yours, when you repeat them, like dada, mamma, and baba.

Most babies are glad to be upright in a sitting position and some of them will be able to sit up by themselves. Some might be rocking on their hands and knees, wanting to crawl.

At this age babies enjoy sensory experiences; different textures, soft toys and colourful objects will hold their attention.

Around this age your baby might start teething and not be themselves. They may be drooling and have swollen gums. Some babies will not be affected by teething, some might be slightly off, but others can cry more and not sleep as well. Sometimes, they are in so much discomfort that they will refuse a bottle or a breast. (more about teething on the page)

Weaning

When you introduce solids at 6 months, your baby is more than ready. How much solids would be enough for your baby?

A 6-month-old baby doesn't need that much to eat; this period is mostly for introducing solid food and different flavours. When you introduce your baby to new tastes and textures while weaning, your baby will tell you what foods they like and dislike.

Remember that milk is still the main source of nutrition, so your baby should always be offered milk before solids until they reach month 8. When you are starting to wean, start with only one meal a day; there is no need to give your baby more than one ounce per feed. Slowly, you can increase that if the baby loves solid foods up to 3 ounces 3 times. There is no need to rush, take your baby's lead.

Some babies are more interested in solids than others but keep introducing them and be consistent. Remember, this is another new skill for them, so keep on trying. The longer your baby has been on solids, the more likely it is that they will be interested in solids. This skill, like any other, requires consistency and patience.

Start solids with pureed fruits or veggies, whole-grain cereal, and full-fat yoghurt. Every food should be introduced every 3 to 4 days, and you should look for allergic reactions. Avocado, banana, sweet potato, pear, butternut squash, broccoli, brown rice cereal, and oatmeal baby cereal are just examples of the most common foods that we can start weaning with.

Nowadays, finger food is also given to babies; many parents like baby-led weaning, instead of feeding them on a spoon, you let your baby explore the tasty food on their own; this way, you give your baby a chance to feed themselves independently.

When choosing baby-led weaning make sure that pieces are soft and small-sized pieces, it will be easier for your baby to chew on and it will be easier to digest. Here are some examples: steamed potatoes, sweet potatoes, green beans, broccoli, fine chopped pears, peaches and strawberries, and small pieces of cheese.

No sugar or salt should be added to your baby's food, but spices are welcome. Please keep it simple. You want your baby to experience every flavour, and one at a time is enough for now.

Once you start solids, start offering your baby water. It is also good to know not to offer too much water, as your baby's little tummy might get full. Give your baby 4 to 8 oz of water a day. This amount will be enough, and they will still have space to have full feeds on breastmilk, formula, or solids.

Solids might affect your baby's digestion. Solids are more complex to digest. I would advise you to avoid solid food before bed, as it might affect their sleep. The last solid meal should be at least one hour before bed. But with this age, I would keep it simple and give solids at lunch, and once your baby is adapted to solids, increase the feed.

With solids introduced, your baby also might get gassy, leading to a fussy baby who might not sleep as well as they used to.

Your baby might need more frequent nappy changes now that they are on solids, and their poop will look different than when they were only on milk.

At 6 months of age, breast milk no longer contains much iron. Your baby will need protein and iron in their food from 6 months onward.

This will keep your baby full for longer and allow them to sleep for longer stretches. When you are starting to introduce protein, please offer it during lunchtime so they will have enough time to digest it.

Your baby will soon start crawling, so please ensure that some games you play are on their tummy. Also, practise sitting with cushions all over the floor so it is a safe and soft landing if your baby rolls down. It is perfect time to practise standing, as we need to activate these little chunky legs and use the leg muscles to prepare them for crawling. Your baby's teeth might now be visible. Oh, what a joy in that little grin.

Handling Disruptions: Managing Teething

Teething is a long process; your baby might look like they are teething for weeks, but there are no teeth in sight. Good news is that your baby will not feel the same discomfort with every tooth coming out.

A study said that teething symptoms come in an 8-day window: 4 days before the tooth emerges, 1 day when it erupts and 3 days after. I find this interesting, as babies who starting to teethe are showing signs of teething for weeks.

How Can You Help?

- Chewing on something cold will reduce pain and inflammation when your baby has sore gums.
- Use your finger to massage their gums. Offer a teething toy or a chilled washcloth. Don't give the baby frozen things; they might get frostbite on their gums.

- Nighttime can be highly challenging when teething. Before bedtime, dip your clean finger in cool water before the last feed, gently apply pressure and massage the areas. This will reduce pain before eating and might reduce the chance that your baby will wake up due to hunger.
- Give lots of reassurance and comfort but stick to the routine. If they have shorter naps, make sure that you move bedtime 20 minutes earlier. You don't want them to be overtired when teething, as this will again make it difficult for them to settle.

Sample of 6 Months Old Sleep and Feeding Schedule is same as 5 months old one. Check above.

“A well-spent day brings happy sleep.”

Leonardo da Vinci

Chapter 8

Baby Sleep (7-9 Months)

Transitioning From 3 Naps to 2

Between 7 – 8 months, your baby will start to show signs that they are ready to transition from 3 naps to 2. You will know that they are ready if they are sleeping shorter at night, having shorter naps, or resisting that third nap.

This is one of the hardest nap transitions and might take you up to 4 weeks to adjust properly, some babies are very adaptable and will be able to adjust sooner.

When transitioning from 3 naps to 2 make sure that they have no more than 3 hours of sleep during the day. You will decide how long the naps will be, but I tend to suggest one hour nap in the morning and 2 hours nap in the afternoon. In the perfect world both naps should be in the cot, but if
that is not doable, make sure that one of them is in the cot.

Ideal 7-to-12 Month Sleep Routine

Wake up
2.5 hours awake
Nap 1
3 hours awake
Nap 2
3.5 hours awake
Bedtime

Seven Months Old

Baby on the Move

Your baby has reached 7 months. If you still need to make your house and area where they spend most of the time childproof, now is the time. Make sure that all the delicate and breakable things, as well as cables, are out of reach. Pay attention to what is on the floor; make sure the floor is clear of any tiny pieces, as this can be a choking hazard for your baby now that they are putting everything in their mouth. They are moving fast, and their activity has reached another level. They are on the go, getting smarter, stronger, and more independent.

Food

Your baby now has two to three meals of solid food each day, but their primary food is still milk, whether you are breastfeeding or formula feeding. Please make sure that your baby is eating clean and unprocessed food. Foods that contain sugar and salt should be avoided. Honey, unpasteurised raw food, and cow's milk are no-goes.

Fruit, vegetables, and whole grains are still the best, as well as full-fat yoghurt. If your baby isn't allergic to food, it is time to introduce the eggs. Eggs are great. Eggs are a great source of protein and vitamin D and B12. When introducing them, pay attention to any allergic reactions. Remember, introduce new foods with a 3-4-day gap, especially when introducing high-allergenic food.

Sleep

Early wakings, the baby refusing to have the third nap, the third nap becoming so short, and difficulty falling asleep, are all signs that your baby is ready to transition from 3 to 2 naps. Transition from 3 to 2 naps a day if all the naps are very short, around 45 minutes. 45-minute naps indicate that you must extend that waking window, so drop that third nap. Waking window for this age is between 2.5 -3.5 hours

Once your baby transitioned from 3 to 2 naps a day, you will have more time and more freedom; you can start attending the activities and classes.

7 month old babies should have 3 hours of sleep during the day broken into 2 naps. If your baby is now having 2 naps, make sure that the first nap of the day is between 1 and 2 hours, and that nap is no longer than 2 hours. A longer first nap might cause the baby not to want a second nap. Naps that are longer than 2 hours, can cause early wakings. If the first nap has been short, the baby still has a chance to catch up on sleep in that second nap

If you still think your baby is not ready to drop the third nap, please ensure that your baby is awake by 3.30 pm.

You will get more sleep now. Your baby is on solids, and their tummy has been used to it, which will affect their sleep patterns, especially overnight. Expect long stretches of sleep.

Your little one might be rolling on their tummy, which might now become their go-to sleeping position; let them know it is okay if they can roll over to their back by themselves. When you put them down to sleep, still make sure you put them down on their back.

All the support and playing sessions with you fully present, will now pay off; when the baby feels emotionally supported and happy, all the challenges that come with sleep can decrease.

Development

Your baby is now sitting independently. If they haven't started yet or have tried to crawl but not quite done it, don't worry, give them some time, this is coming your way. Every baby is different; some babies skip crawling or develop their own technique, which is okay. We all are aware of all different styles involving crawling. What sort of crawling will happen in your house? If you watch your baby closely, you might have noticed their motor and fine motor skills are also improving. Your baby might be able to pick up things, especially small objects, using a pointy finger and thumb. Please keep those small pieces out of reach.

At 7 months, your baby is super chatty, trying to make sounds and copy your voice as they babble away. Don't limit their curious exploring adventures; keep them safe, but let them move, explore, and be. If they are struggling, don't just jump in; pause and watch them, allowing them to figure things out independently. If the baby is starting to get very frustrated, go on and help them. You want your baby to practise problem solving skills

Playtime

Lift-up, colourful, and mirror books are excellent for this age. Different-coloured scarves are also excellent. Toys are fun, but the things we have in the kitchen that are safe to use will be even better. Push-button toys that light up will be another great hit. Sensory toys, what's in the box or a bag, playing stacking blocks and nursery rhymes with actions will also keep your little one busy and focused.

Sample 7-12 Months Old Sleep and Feeding Schedule	
Time	Activity
7.00 am	Wake up, feed
7.30 am	Breakfast, play
9.30 am	Nap 1 (1-1.5 hours)
11.00 am	Wake up, feed, play
12.00 pm	Lunch
2.00 pm	Nap 2 (1-1.5hours)
3.30 pm	Wake up, feed playtime
5.00 pm	Dinner, low key activity
6.30 pm	Bath and bedtime routine
6.45 pm	Feed
7.00 pm	Bedtime

Eight Months Old

Food

Your baby is now an expert in solids but still drinking milk. At this age 3 meals should be in place Your baby at this age should have 2-3 meals plus one healthy snack.

Try adding finger food with different textures to your baby's diet. Now is the time to introduce a baby to the dining table and let your baby join family meals; this way, you are fostering good eating habits. After 8 months, you can start offering solids before milk and gradually replace them. Let's start with lunch.

If you haven't already, you should introduce your baby to drinking from a sipping cup. The first few tries might be difficult, and they will end up playing with the cup more than anything else, but soon, they will pick up on the technique. Remember, practise, practise, and more practise.

Sleep

Eight-month-olds could wake up more frequently, but that is due to their development; they are now developing new motor skills. Pulling themselves up is one of the exciting new skills your baby is starting to be good at.

The sleeping schedule, naps, and bedtime routine are still the same. If you have a bumpy few days, please stick to the schedule regardless. Your baby now has two naps a day. The wake window is between 2.5 and 3.5 hours. You might notice that your baby prefers one parent when it comes to bedtime.

They will also be more active in their sleep, hence working hard on their skills during the waking window.

Development

At 8 months your baby is becoming a fantastic observer. They are aware of their surroundings, and they take it all in like a little sponge. Your baby is watching and learning.

I am sure you have already noticed that whenever your baby can see you, they will cry. Separation anxiety is kicking in. Your baby might cry when you say goodbye; they miss you. Please do not hide or leave without saying goodbye. Make sure that goodbyes are short, and don't send mixed signals, as you might prolong their being upset. Clinginess, shyness, and separation anxiety are expected at this age.

Use the same sentence every time you leave and say goodbye; that sentence will signal your baby that you are coming back. Whoever is caring for your baby will be able to distract them and stop them crying once you leave.

Your baby is sitting perfectly steady, and their muscles are getting stronger. All the action is happening on the floor while the baby is in constant motion. They will be rolling, crouching, twisting, and rocking while kneeling, how impressive. By now your baby might already be crawling. If your baby is not crawling yet, don't worry; they will get there. Practice makes perfect.

Make sure that they are practising this during the waking window.

Talking is another superpower that a baby is now developing. Your baby should be able to start putting some words together, like "mamma" and "dada." Your baby might not be able to say them, but they can still understand what the words mean.

Play

Play games to help your baby realise that you are here even if they don’t see you. Play peek-a-boo, cover the toys with muslin, and then take them off so they can see them again.

Texture and shapes will keep your baby busy. Read to your baby, sing to them, and encourage early language skills as they are about to start forming their first words.

Nine Months Old

Food

Your baby can now practise how to drink from a cup and how to drink from a bottle with a straw in it. Let's activate all the muscles that are needed when your baby starts talking. 9 month old babies need solids 3 times a day plus healthy snacks and milk of course.

Sleep

The wake-up window is now a minimum of 2.5 hours to 3.5 hours. Your baby will have two naps. Daily naps should be no more than 3 hours in total. If it is more than that, it could affect your nights or cause frequent wakings during the night.

If your baby needs more than 20 minutes to fall asleep, extend your waking window by 5-10 minutes. The ideal time for your baby to fall asleep would be 5-20 minutes.
Also, make sure that your baby is not too tired, as that might also affect their sleep.

Development

Your baby is now 9 months old. They are standing and sitting for long periods of time, they might lift themselves
up and hold furniture while trying to walk. They are clapping and can hold their own bottle, what a grown-up baby!

Your baby now understands words like mumma, bottle, dada, milk, and snack.

Play

Perfect toys for this age are walkers that push, tunnels, and balls, and of course there is a whole range of unique and diverse toys; but babies love when you throw the ball, and they will rush to get it.
This is the time where you can sing a songs and clap to the rhythm, so they can show off these clapping skills they have just learned.

"Sleep is the investment for the energy you need tomorrow."

Robert Glazer

Chapter 9

Baby Sleep (10-12 Months)

Ten Months Old

Food

At this age eating habits of your baby might change. Their rapid growth suddenly will slow down, and they might be less interested in food and have less milk. This is normal. Don't stress if their weight is still following the chart.

Sleep

You baby is continuing having two naps a day, before and after lunch. Wake windows will be 3.5 hours, but they could likely tolerate a bit more + 30 min. The wake window is not that important, anymore; I suggest you form your set schedule and stick to it, followed by the baby's sleep.

If your baby has fallen asleep in the buggy or a car, when it is not their time to sleep, it will be challenging to put them in bed as they might wake up and resettling at this point will not happen.

You will notice that this might happen in the mornings, if it happens adjust the afternoon nap accordingly. If your baby has fallen asleep in the afternoon, please don’t let them sleep past 4pm.

Sleep might be affected more than ever at 8-10 months if you haven't had a routine and schedule in place, this is the time where it would be harder to break old habits.

The sleeping patterns of your baby might be different as they are going through separation anxiety and crawling. They might fight these naps, or it becomes difficult to put them down, and you might be wondering if you should drop that morning nap; I suggest you don't. You don't want to end up with a cranky, overtired baby who is already having separation anxiety.

This is 10 months of sleep regression; they are maturing, crawling, and saying words, understand this is again one significant milestone for them. Big developmental progression is also sleeping regression.

Developmental

Your baby is now big. They are all over the place, crawling and eating all by themselves. Your baby is happy to be able to move finally, but boy, they are always on the go! They love it when you interact and play with them. They are pushing themselves up and might be able to take their first step.

Separation anxiety is kicking in more than ever when they are going through all these big emotions. Routine will give them stability and comfort. Also, make sure to have plenty of cuddles and kisses during the day to stay connected.

This is also a time when Mummy is their focus. You can't leave them alone or with anyone else because they are so attached. Some babies at this age don't want to go to anyone but you.

I adore this age as they still need you, hence the separation anxiety. But they also crave independence; they're a little daredevil, exploring every corner of your home. They're everywhere, in cupboards, drawers, and laundry baskets. Let them explore but keep a watchful eye.

You might notice that your baby can't focus on one thing for long. They keep on jumping from one thing to another. This is because your baby wants to be involved in everything. They want to do it all, but even slight noise in the background can distract them. They will stop what they are doing and want to go and check what this noise is all about, where is it coming from, what's going on.

.

Eleven Months Old

Food

When they are eating, they want to do it on their own. Your
baby will continue having 3 meals per day plus an additional 2 healthy snacks, and of course milk.

Sleep

Your baby might start showing you the signs that they are ready for the transition from 2 naps a day to 1, but I would wait until 12 months to do that.

Transitioning to only one nap means your baby will have big 5 hour wake windows. Most of the 11-month-olds are not ready for that yet. If you push the transition too early, before your baby is ready, you will come across other sleeping challenges like early morning rising or frequent wakings at night.

Ensure your baby has two naps of at most 3 hours. No longer than one hour at a maximum in the morning and two hours in the afternoon. Baby's ideal bedtime at this age is somewhere between 7 and 8 pm.

You should put your baby to bed around 6.30 pm only if some of the following happen during the day.

- Your baby didn't sleep for some reason in the afternoon
- The afternoon nap was short
- Your baby had less than 2 hours of sleep during the day

Development

At this age, your baby is standing on their own, and they might be taking their first steps on their own as well, moving like a little ninja and cruising around furniture.

Your little one is active, you might need to have that second coffee in hand, as you might feel exhausted before lunch. Your baby often throws their toys and reaches for hidden toys, such as under the table or under the chair.

To help your baby start walking or practise walking, bring out all those wheely toys, baby pushchairs, and push-and-pull toys. Activity toys that your baby can push around the house will also be great. Remember ride-on toys are lots of fun too.

Bare feet are the best for walking, but if you are out and about, it may be time for your baby to have some slippers that will protect their little feet. If your baby is walking, I highly suggest a pre-walker shoe as they are soft and give your baby the support that they need.

Play

If you want to keep your baby occupied and happy, please give them a ball and also play with them, rolling the ball back and forth. They will be mesmerised by the ball's movement. Ensure you have some kitchen stuff that they can play with when you are in the kitchen. Make sure that plastic balls, boxes, and spoons are all safe to play with. Also, turn the music up and sing those nursery rhymes.

This is also a time when you can introduce role-play toys. Stacking boxes and simple puzzles will also keep them occupied.

Twelve Months Old
Happy 1st Birthday!

You might not believe it, but your baby has turned 1. Congratulations! You have done an amazing job. You are now stepping together with your little one into toddlerhood. How exciting.

Sleep

Your baby is now sleeping through the night, having still 2 naps in the day which you can now slowly start to transition into one nap. If your baby is not ready just yet cut that first nap to half. So, if your baby had a 1-hour morning nap make sure that now it is only 30 minutes. I find this works wonders. Transition is never easy. Then, when they are ready cut that 30-minute nap and just leave time for a long afternoon nap after lunch.

Development

Your baby, now toddler, will love to do things on their own, they will want to do it all by themselves. But on the other hand, they will want dependence. This is the time when you will notice this dependence/independence, "I want you but don't want you" stage.

Play

This is a perfect time to introduce crayons and start colouring books and stickers

.

Your newborn toddler will maybe start pulling your hair, try to keep their fingers busy with toys.

Also engage your toddler in walking activities, practise that part and make them tired, as they will sleep through the night.

Transitioning From 2 Naps to 1

Transitioning from 2 naps to 1, usually happens between 12 – 14 months of age. Signs your baby is ready to transition to only one nap include early wakings, short naps.

Your baby is growing, not a baby anymore. By turning one, overnight they become toddler. Lots of things are happening for them when they turn 1. Sleep transition will shift from morning and afternoon nap to just one nap, midday. This change will be a big leap as your toddler will now have to stay awake for 5 hours. To make the change easier, I recommend gradually shortening the morning nap by 30 minutes shorter. Have a week adjustment for every 30 minutes based on the length of morning nap. After the nap make sure that the waking window is 4.5 hours before bedtime

Total daytime sleep should be no more than 2.5 hours, this is a perfect amount of sleep for most toddlers at this age.

Ideal 12 Months + Wake Window Schedule

Wake up
5 hours awake
Nap 1
4. 5hours awake
Bedtime

Sample 12+ Month Old Sleeping and Feeding Schedule	
Time	**Activity**
7 am	Wake up, milk
7.30 am	Breakfast, then activity
10 am	Snack
12 pm	Lunch
12.30 pm	Nap (1.5 – 2hours)
2.30 pm	Wake up, snack, playtime
5.30 pm	Dinner, followed by gentle activity
6.30 pm	Bath and bedtime routine
7.00 pm	Milk
7.30 pm	Bedtime

"There's no way to be a perfect mother, and a million ways to be a good one."

Jill Churchill

Chapter 10

Prioritising Mothers' Well Being

Nurturing Self-Care and Balance

We have now reached one great chapter, which may be the most significant part of this book. This story I will share with you is very personal and has a special place in my heart. It is a story involving one of my clients who made me aware that mothers out there suffer in silence; mothers who appear to be well and good and keep their feelings to themselves. Without you, Mummy, all that's written in this book wouldn't have any sense or wouldn't be possible. Your well-being is the most important thing you can give yourself, your little ones, and your family.

No feeling is too much; open up and share your feelings. If you need to ask for help, it is OK. Remember, in the past, we had a village that raised our children; now, it is only you and your partner. It is OK not to feel OK.

This chapter is dedicated not just to my clients but to all the mothers out there who are carrying all these feelings that the rest of us might never see. It should remind all of us that, in today's world, we are more connected than ever, but we are profoundly disconnected, so many mothers feel alone and need help.

I am incredibly grateful to my client for letting me share her story with you. This is not just her story; I think that this is a call to all of us to pay attention, offer a hand, and listen to the silent struggles mothers have to go through.

Dear Mummy, I hope you feel connected as you read this chapter and find the strength to speak out if needed. The best stories are the ones that come from the heart.

Recognising the Importance of Mothers' Well Being

On a December evening, during a casual dinner, a dear friend reached out to me. She asked if I could assist a local mother battling mastitis and feeling poorly. It was a request that caught me off guard, as I had long-stopped working nights. Yet, against all odds, I found myself saying yes. Looking back, I can't help but feel it was meant to be.

I arrived at the client's house at 9 pm. I rang the bell, and this graceful, gentle lady opened the door. She was in her 30s, I thought. Despite her health struggles, she wore the most beautiful smile and invited me in. We walked to the kitchen, where she was having her dinner. Her husband was there, listening, I could feel he was supportive; he just wanted his wife to have a good night's rest.

They had been sleeping in separate rooms since the baby was born. I understand, he thought they would get better sleep if they slept separately.

While she was eating, I met her baby boy. He was 4 months old and sleeping peacefully in Moses basket.

He had perfect little features. I gathered all the information I needed about the baby for the night.

Once she had told me everything, I asked her, "And how are you?" she said, she was fine, and I remembered thinking, “she doesn't seem poorly." I was immediately ashamed of myself for just thinking that thought.

After she finished her dinner, I gently insisted it was time for us to take her upstairs to rest. Then I saw a slight hesitation, but she had gathered everything needed, and we went upstairs.

I was sleeping in the room with the baby, and she slept next door. We said goodnight and agreed that I would bring her baby boy to her when he woke up for a feed. The way she said goodnight, I knew there was more to it. I could feel her voice becoming quieter and wobbly. Before she shut that door, I whispered, "If you need me, I am here; please remember that." She smiled warmly, her gratitude shining through, and slowly closed the door.

We all know babies are very noisy sleepers, but not her baby. He was the quietest baby I have ever encountered. I had to keep checking to see if he was breathing. That night, he slept well and was very settled with me.

When he was ready to feed, I took him next door to his mother for a feed. I would sit on the floor while the mother fed her baby; we had the loveliest chats about motherhood and the smell of newborns. I loved every single moment of it. Her stories were warm, and our chats in that big attic room were magical.

I listened carefully to everything she said, and I could feel her opening up to me more with every word. I could see her being so vulnerable, gentle and lonely. She was lost and overwhelmed; she just needed a companion, she needed to be heard, and she needed support without judgement, support that she didn't get, or was too scared to open about as society says motherhood is amazing.

It is I agree, but there are mothers out there who are really struggling. We all have been there when you can't fall asleep at night, overthinking, when all your feelings surface and anxiety kicks in. At night, often we hear our thoughts so loudly, they hurt. I could feel her processing all the feelings and thoughts yet being so grateful for me just being there with her.

The next morning, I took the baby downstairs to his dad. He was having breakfast with his two-year-old brother. I said goodbye and left. Dad made sure that Mummy had a rest that morning.

Later that day, I got a message: "Thank you so much for coming to our rescue last night. It was reassuring to have you there; I haven't slept so well for days! You are lovely, and my baby boy is very settled with you."

Only 5 days later, I received a phone call from my client's Mum to say that her daughter had been taken to hospital and asked if I could come back to help her through the night. I said, of course, and arranged the night that would suit her best.

I arrived at the house at 8 pm. That night, my client opened the door, and she greeted me with a big smile once again. Only this time, I could see the pain and sadness in her eyes. She looked very fragile. We headed to the kitchen, chatted, and headed upstairs for the night. But before she could close the door, I held her hand and whispered, "I am here." She nodded gently and closed the door.

Not long after, I heard a knock on the door. It was her. She looked at me and said, "I need you." I followed her into her bedroom, leaving the door of the room where the baby was, open. She was shaking, out of breath, and not well. “Poor thing,” I thought.

That night in that big attic room, I felt an incredible connection with this mother, whom I knew little about but understood so profoundly.

She was shaking and hyperventilating. She held my hand tightly like she didn't want to let go. I led her to her bed, made sure she was lying down and covered her with a duvet. Only then I realised she wasn't cold; she was having a panic attack.

Calmly, I said, "It's okay. I'm here." I let her feel her body and her feelings without any judgement. Slowly stroking her arm, I calmly asked her to tell me about her happiest memory with her husband, and she immediately lit up. She started talking about festivals they used to go to and how much fun that was. While talking about it, her breathing slowed down, and her shaking stopped.

I looked at her. She was so incredibly strong and fragile at the same time. She is so brave, I thought. I looked at her while she started drifting off and thought about how much I admired her at that moment. She had put down all her walls. She was so pure, so amazingly honest about what she was going through. There was no judgement in this room, and she felt safe. She drifted off to sleep, knowing that I was was going to be just next door.

Once she was asleep, I left the room.

Afterwards, we had a long chat. I told her how important it was to address how she was feeling and that if she needed help, she should seek it. I also told her about magical hug therapy and how important it is to take some time in a day for herself. (more about the hug therapy in chapter 12)

Then I told myself I needed to do something about this. I have seen mothers who have struggled and needed support, but this Mum was so special to me.

There are so many new mothers out there who need support, but they are ashamed and scared of what people will think of them. They put that brave face on for a baby, husband, and family but inside, they are falling apart, thinking repeatedly about what is wrong with them. Some of them are lucky enough to have husbands who notice, and they open and seek help. Some of them have a friend that they can talk to about it. Some of them have their close family members nearby. But some.... have nobody, they would feel all the burden on their shoulders and not be able to open up. Some of them struggle and will struggle for up to two years. Some of them never make it to their child's 1st birthday as they have been walking alone.

A week later, I received her message saying she was practising hug therapy. Her husband had moved back to her room, and she was feeling much better. She had also started swimming once a week, which she has always enjoyed.

I was over the moon for her; I was so happy she was brave enough to vocalise to her husband that she needed him by her side at night.

She implemented hug therapy in the comfort of her home with the people that she loves the most. She didn't need to change a lot, she needed to start taking baby steps towards her recovery. These baby steps have led her to significant steps in therapy; she admitted to herself 4 months later that she needed professional help, and she has prioritised that. I am so incredibly proud of her.

She has bloomed. She has stepped on the journey to heal herself. I know that wasn't easy for her, but healing has become her priority—to be better and kinder to herself, to love herself more.

Some mothers would die for their children. I wanted to remind them to live for their children. There is so much to this sentence; read it again.

If our society were more understanding about what mothers in the first year are going through, if they would not judge but instead support them, mothers would feel comfortable enough to say how they feel. They need a listening ear, a shoulder to lean on, or just someone to be there. They are resilient warriors, but they are also humans; they are newborns as well. When a baby is born, so is the mother.

I want to remind every mother reading this that asking for help is not a sign of weakness; it's a sign of immense strength. Acknowledging when we need support takes courage and is a step closer to healing and self-care. Step closer to living for your baby.

"Any man can be a father, but it takes someone special to be a dad."

Anne Geddes

Chapter 11

Father's Role

When I think of my life, I look back and reflect. I had the most beautiful childhood. My upbringing was memorable, filled with love, positivity, laughter, and an 'I can do' spirit. As I have mentioned before, my Mum was a single mother but gave me all she could. Our bond was very special then, and so it is until this day.

My Mum went above and beyond to support me and to make me feel special. In the eighties being a child of divorced parents was frowned upon. Mum knew that my school days were challenging, sometimes not only by my peers, but more so from my teachers. I have never let school affairs affect me as I knew I was heard and supported at home. Mum and I had a relationship where I could talk openly about everything (except co-sleeping as I knew how much that meant to her), she has taught me many things that I will be forever grateful for. Now that I am an adult, she is my best friend, rock, and shoulder to cry on.

You have maybe noticed that I am talking about my mum a lot, but where is my dad? My parents separated when I was 9 months old, so he wasn't involved, he wasn't there, and he wasn't that much interested in me. My dad was *never* there for me; maybe he didn't know how to be a dad, like many Balkan men of his time.

My grandpa had never showed him love. Because of that, my dad didn't have a template for what a 'dad' should do. In the countryside of Croatia, in the past, parents raised boys into men. These boys needed to be men from the very start and of course boys don't 'cry' or 'talk' about their feelings. Men of that generation have struggled to express their emotions because nobody has shown them how. 'Strong' and 'tough' were adjectives that were used to describe little boys.

Even without my father being there for me, I was lucky enough to be raised by my uncle and my amazing grandad (mum's side). They were not just my father figures, but they were my teachers, my role models. When they took me under their wing, they showed me how men can love and showed me that a father is not just biological. I was lucky enough to have two unique male figures to raise me. I have never lacked male love; I was blessed with double the love.

My dear uncle and my amazing grandfather have shown me the masculine side, which remains solid and dominant in my life.

Sadly, they are no longer with us, but their spirits are always with me. Their compassion and understanding and guidance have shaped me into the person I am today. I will be forever grateful for all the love they showered upon me. They gave me the love that I have never received from my dad.

To this day, I feel sorry for my dad. He has never had a chance or taken the time to get to know me. He never knew how to love. I only got harsh criticism from him and his side of the family.

Sadly, his unhappiness and lack of connection and communication have had an impact on our lives, on our bond.

Did I try to connect, yes, many times, but his upbringing is so deeply engraved. I can't change my dad and his views on fatherhood. But I see changes, as the fathers these days want to be involved.

Embrace the Journey of Parenthood

Dear Dads, please don't wait until your child is old enough to take them to the places of your interests and hobbies. Your baby is here, and they need you now and so does your partner. Being a dad doesn't mean just doing fun things, being a dad means doing the hard things as well. As your baby is growing and you are taking on the challenges that comes with parenthood, you will learn so much about yourself, mostly when you interact with your baby.

I promise you that after your baby is born, you will find a new purpose in life. Will it be big and bright? Oh yes, but with tough patches. You will also experience a love that you have never experienced before and your baby will also add about two years to your life expectancy, according to science.

Fathers might not be able to breastfeed, but when it comes to language development, they have a huge role to play. Babies and toddlers need fathers to learn greater vocabulary.

Mothers on other hand often change their language, once they have a baby, mothers tend to simplify their speech to help baby to understand them easier.

Father involvement in a baby's life is crucial. So dear Father, embrace this time with your baby and partner, please know that your presence and efforts make a such a difference.

Mothers and Fathers Equally Important

I must admit that every time I pass a father who is involved in their child's life, some kind of warmth comes over me. I never had this as a child. This is how it should be.

The concept of fatherhood has evolved at top speed over the past 25 years. I have witnessed the changes since I started working in childcare. These changes are drastic in such a wonderful way.

Today, dads are much more involved and emotionally present in their children's lives. This positive shift has greatly impacted children's perception of their fathers, particularly for boys who need positive male role models. It makes such a difference when that role model is at home fully involved, fully present, as is very often the case nowadays.

This change didn't happen overnight. Mothers are also hugely responsible for this; mothers have started embracing it. They have started learning to accept help and step back. They have started to enjoy and appreciate time away from their babies. They have started enjoying the break as they know they are coming back refreshed and recharged.

Dads are no longer just providers, they now take parental leave, which was uncommon in the past; not heard of in the culture where I was born.

As I have mentioned before, it is heartwarming to witness this change, where parents work together to raise their children, making decisions together while growing as a family.

Mother nature has an amazing way of creating roles in your child's development. Both parents are essential; they don't have the same role, but different roles that complement each other.

According to Dr Anna Machin's research, mothers and fathers each bring unique contributions to their child's upbringing.

Mother's role is to support their child's emotional state, providing comfort, security and nurturing. Mothers are biologically switched on to respond to their babies' needs. All thanks to the high level of oxytocin. Oxytocin 'love hormone' helps to create that strong emotional bond between Mother and baby, that bond is critical for the child's emotional development and sense of security.

Fathers will bond with their baby through interaction. Dr. Machin's research put a limelight on fathers' involvement in activities such a rough-and-tumble play. This will become important around 6 months of the baby's life. This is not just fun for fathers, it's just as much fun for babies too. That rough play is essential for the child's physical and cognitive development. This also helps your baby to learn about boundaries, develop problem-solving skills, and understand social interactions.

Let's wrap this up, both mothers and fathers are so needed in a child's life. Embracing their own individual roles and working together will ensure that children receive the diverse support that they need to thrive. Giving both parents a chance to engage deeply with their baby can lead to a fulfilling parenting experience for both parents.

Fathers and Their New Role Struggles

Many new fathers are quite often wondering if their feelings should be taken into consideration. Yes, they should! As you have stepped into a new role as a parent, you are going through new experiences, and believe it or not, your hormonal levels will change. This baby of yours will change your life forever for the better.

I am sure that becoming a dad is exciting, but nothing can prepare you for what lies ahead. Traditionally, fathers have been providers, while mothers have stayed at home, caring for their children.

Many fathers see themselves as head of the family, protectors and problem solvers, the ones who can fix things. But then this lovely baby arrives, they might feel lost and down, as there is not much they can do. They can't soothe the baby as mothers can; they can't breastfeed... This is when reality kicks in, and many fathers feel helpless. But just being there for your family is enough.

When it comes to bonding, most fathers have this big expectation that they will fall in love from day one. But be prepared, not every dad will immediately feel that bond with their baby; that is normal. Give it some time. Some dads bond later, the adjustment period can be challenging.

When the baby arrives, male testosterone levels drop, making dads less likely to engage in risky behaviours and they become more nurturing towards their newborn. These changes happen when dads are actively involved and spend one-on-one time with their babies during the first year.

A good friend of mine described fatherhood to me: "For the first year of my baby's life, I wasn't aware I was the father; I had no clue what I was doing." Many dads can relate to this. Until the baby is a solid chunk who can move, many don't know how to approach the baby.

Despite this, dads are involved and supportive in today's world. They might not be able to give the same level of care and support to babies as mothers do, but Mother Nature gave them other superpowers.

Practical Advice to New Fathers; How to be Supportive to New Mothers

Fathers, I would like to address your importance and impact when you are just there for your partner after your child's birth.

The postpartum period is extremely important. The first 6 weeks after giving birth is time when your partner's body needs to heal and rest.

Many cultures had other people caring only for mothers during that period. The village ensures the mother is OK, and then they know the baby will be OK, too. Sadly, we don't live in a world where the family is nearby. Daddy, this is where you step in. You are about to become that village.

Your partner has been on this long 9-month journey carrying your baby. During pregnancy, her body goes through incredible transformations. It is not just that her body and brain changes - her level of hormones will go out of the roof. After birth, her body goes through changes again.

After giving birth, mother is also born, not only does she have to deal with her new baby, but she has to cope with; body aches, swollen breasts, vaginal pain and haemorrhoids, hair loss and so on.

She is about to feel all the rainbow of emotions. Excitement, anxiety, exhaustion, sleepiness and depression. This big emotion will settle. But sometimes they don't, and extreme changes in hormones can lead to mood swings or "baby blues".

It is essential that if your partner is getting worse, feeling down all the time, you seek help. Please bear in mind that postpartum depression is an actual thing.

You should be aware of the signs or symptoms. Don't be scared to ask for help if needed. Here is the website that will give you support: https://pandasfoundation.org.uk they are not there just for your partner or a wife. They are there for fathers as well.

The arrival of your baby will change everything. You will no longer be that number one. Your little bundle of joy is taking that limelight and is not going anywhere for the next 18 years.

When you become a parent, you are entering a whole new world and starting from scratch. It is important to communicate openly with your partner. Be honest with yourself and your partner about your feelings and experiences. Being there for her will encourage her to open up. You are both in this together, and you must both be active members to become the best parents for your baby.

Take time off during these first precious weeks, when your presence and responsiveness will be so much appreciated. Together, you will work out what works best for you and your baby. Your active participation in these early stages is critical to your family's future well-being. This time is not for shutting each other out. This is the time when teamwork will pay off.

Sometimes fathers come across as non-supportive and distant. Bear in mind that for a man it is not always easy to admit that he is losing control, he is feeling like he can't fix things, he is also dealing with a lot on the inside. Until now he was a problem solver, but babies don't come with a manual.

Keeping Intimacy Alive

After baby's arrival your intimacy will change. This drastic change might seem like intimacy is drifting away, which can put strain on a relationship. Partly this is due to your partner's tiredness and hormonal changes. New dads must understand that baby's arrival takes lots of physical and emotional energy. They must understand that baby will be the centre of attention, especially in the first few months.

Many new dads will be experiencing rejection after a baby, but intimacy can still be present in your new chapter. This part is all about communication and reconnection. Both parents are learning how to 'be' in their new roles. Embracing each other needs can deeper bond with your partner. Love doesn't wannish after having a baby, it transforms.

Creating a Supportive Environment:

When baby arrives, you will have to juggle many things, but most of all you will have to find a healthy balance between caring for your baby, your partner and yourself. Babies have needs: they need food, sleep, security, and love to thrive.

New mothers need rest and help with breastfeeding. Breastfeeding, especially in the first days is exhausting and stressful, when your partner struggle with breastfeeding, they might feel like they are failing. Stay supportive be there helping her with positioning, changing nappy if needed, or just hand her a baby when she wants to breast feed.

You can also help her by taking care of your newborn while she is resting. Help with feedings. Bottle feeding your baby is great way to start to create bond and don't forget, skin to skin has a amazing bonding benefits.

I would recommend for you to interact with baby when they are full and happy for 20- 30 min. That will give you chance to get to know them. The more you know your baby the better you will understand their needs and you will be able to intuitively respond to them.

"Don't die for your kids, live for them instead."

Paul Watkins

Chapter 12

Connection and Well-being Techniques That I Swear by

In my 25 years in childcare, I have picked up techniques that few discuss and implement in everyday life and work. These techniques can be beneficial for sleep-deprived parents to find balance and a deeper connection with their partner and baby. These techniques have significantly improved my well-being. I have tried and tested them first. When I saw their impact on me, I started to share them with my friends and then pass them on to my clients, who are parents. It might not everyone's cup of the, but I shared them anyway. However, parents who decided to use them saw the benefits very soon.

Each technique came to my life at the right time, when I needed it the most.

The first is the power of music, the second is magical hug therapy, and the third one is the language of love. When you understand the language of love, it deepens your connection with partner and, later, with your child. This can be applied when they are older and can speak and express their feelings. We are all so unique and we don't all speak the same language of love. There is one more therapy, and that is water therapy. I only came across this once I started teaching swimming. But let's dive deeper into every single one of them and let me explain my reasons.

Singing

The Healing Power of Music

We are all aware that music and its universal language. Rhythm has been present in human life since the beginning of time, rhythm then turned to music. Music can involve so much joy and healing. I have found singing extremely powerful when looking after a little, wonderfully unique Downs Syndrome boy. I have never sung in public and thought I didn't have a lovely voice.

Then I found myself in the new role of looking after little boy with down syndrome, I become open to so many things. I just wanted to make him happy and safe. We have attended classes called singing and sign, and there and then, I have discovered what impact music has on him and his development.

In this class, through singing and signing, he was able to bloom and communicate; while out of the class, that wasn't the case. He was struggling to express himself. I have seen him react to the music, so instead of talking to him, I have started to sing.

That has changed everything. It was like a magical switch. Singing made him calm and happy, made him confident, and his focus improved. I have seen drastic changes, and singing has become our language.

I remember that first day at sing and sign class when I couldn't hear my voice and felt too shy to sing. But seeing what joy music can bring, now I sing all the time. All thanks to little boy whose world was a better place while we were singing. Looking back, I realise that this singing therapy wasn't only for him; it was beneficial for me as well.

Since that realisation, I have been using singing in all parts of the childcare setting, from newborns to toddlers, nurseries to swimming, and it works every time.

But let's see why. Singing engages the brain's emotional centres, allowing us to express and recognise feelings that might be hard to voice. Singing stimulates the release of endorphins, the "feel-good "chemical that reduces stress and promotes well-being. Singing encourages deep breathing, which activates the nervous system and helps the body relax.

Singing lullabies to your baby can calm and soothe them, helping them feel secure and relaxed. Singing can strengthen the connection between parent and baby. While you sing to your baby, they listen, which allows them to develop their language skills.

Nowadays, I have songs for everything. It is incredible how children respond to music from an early age; I have songs for essential things. Here is what has always been very helpful to me. Good morning song, a song for sleep, a song for bath and one the most important... songs for cutting nails! There is one more song for going out, a song for mealtime, sometimes I would sing all day instead of talking.

I know, weird, but there were times with some families when Mums and I would sing instead of talk to each other. These families were rare, but it was great fun, not just for children but for us adults as well.

There is something special about singing, it lifts our spirits during challenging times. While you are singing, your oxytocin levels increase.

Try to sing... Immediately, you will feel better. When you sing, your babies will respond to you differently, your baby will learn how to process their emotions through music.

Music will open different pathways for your baby later to express and explain their feelings, which will impact how to regulate their emotions.

When you sing the task, there will be no fuss, once you have all these songs in place, there will be no tears or resistance. When I start singing a song about the bath, they are already on the stairs. When I start singing a song about sleep, my charge now gives me the biggest koala hug and lays his little head on my shoulder. He knows it's time for sleep. It is incredible how children respond to music. And how they learn through it.

You will notice that if you are down, your mood will lift when you start singing a song, and if the baby is crying and you start to sing, the baby will calm down. Music is the key to making your long days brighter.

It has been shown that music can improve moods and empower babies and young children by reducing stress levels. That will happen to you as well. Once you start singing, music will lift your spirit, and you will begin to sing more.

Here are the tips about singing:

Incorporate singing into your daily routine, even just for a few minutes, while making coffee, cooking, or in the shower. If you don't feel like singing, put on background music and join in.

When your baby is big enough, from about six months of age, join local singing classes or rhyme time in the library. This is an excellent way to socialise and learn some more nursery rhymes. Your baby will love it, and so will you.

You will be in your baby bubble for the first few months. You are too tired to go out but can have fun at home. Have a random karaoke night with your partner. You can sing only a few songs together; that 'feeling-good' wave will wash over you. Sharing fun moments with your partner will also connect you. It's the small things that make a difference. Sing more.

Hug Therapy

The Power of Touch

We all know that human touch is essential for emotional well-being and connection. Hug therapy came along spontaneously; out of the blue, it came during the Covid period. At that time, I lived alone and longed for human interaction. I witnessed that everyone around me felt the same way. Once we were able to create a bubble with another person, I was the happiest I'd been for a long time. I started to see my friends again. Oh boy, that first hug was long. I have never cried so much. I was excited to feel that hug, closeness, and human touch again.

Since then, I have scraped the surface and dug a bit deeper. And this is what I have found. Hug therapy exists and is costly.

Virginia Satir is a family therapist who prescribes hugs. Her famous sentence is: 'We need four hugs a day for survival. We need eight hugs a day for maintenance. We need twelve hugs a day for growth.'

Since then, I have embraced hugging. Hugs are beneficial for both parties. The power of hugging provides comfort and support, reduces stress, and strengthens relationships. Hugging can alleviate fear in people with low self-esteem. Hugs can have a similar effect to painkillers as they can reduce the perception of pain. That is why when a child gets hurt, they need a hug.

Hug therapy has amazing healing properties for babies and new parents. As I am sure you can tell, parenting can feel lonely and isolated, so why don't you and your partner start the hug therapy from day one of becoming parents?

You can give each other support, comfort and reassurance while reducing feelings of loneliness and isolation. Hugging will release oxytocin, the love hormone, that can also help lower your blood pressure and improve health while reducing stress.

Regular hugs strengthen the emotional bonds and foster a deeper trust and intimacy with your partner. This will be especially helpful in the first weeks of parenthood when you find yourself only caring about the baby. And your relationship is something you don't think about.

Your baby will feel safe and loved when you hug. Hugs also provide a sense of security and comfort. Lots of hugs will promote better sleep.

Practical Tips for Hug Therapy

Your and your partner's hugs will be sincere and heartfelt as you go through the same parenthood process. Nobody will understand you more than your partner, who shares that little sweet baby of yours with you. These hugs can tell more than words ever could. Make a family hug your daily routine. Your whole little family will benefit from it. What a joy!

Languages of Love

Understanding and Applying It

Sleep deprivation is one of the most common factors leading to issues and challenges in the early stages of parenthood. Sleep deprivation affects your everyday life. As a new parent, you don't have much time to socialise and relax, and that can take a toll on your relationship. This is why I would also like you to know the languages of love, this might help you go through rough times smoothly.

A few years back, I came across a book that changed my perspective on love. I was blown away by R. Gray Chapman's book, 5 Love Languages, the secret to love that last. In it, he teaches us how to understand and apply the concepts of love languages.

First, you need to know your language or languages because you can have multiple languages. Then, of course, your partner's one or a few. Once you know them, it allows you to have a more meaningful relationship.

I never knew why many people are in long-term relationships but feel unloved. This book opened my eyes, and I got my answers.

People often show their love through their language of love, but if you don't have the same language of love as your partner, your partner can feel unloved. This for me was mind-blowing! This is powerful!!!

There are 5 Different Languages of Love

1. **Words of Affirmation**

This love language is expressing love through verbal compliments. Words of appreciation can be really uplifting.

2. **Act of Service**

This love language demonstrates love through helpful actions. It is all about action; if you want to show your love, show it through actions.

3. **Receiving Gifts**

Giving and receiving thoughtful gifts to these people symbolises thought and effort. The value of the gifts has nothing to do with this, but the meaning behind them matters.

4. **Quality time**

You are spending meaningful time with your loved ones, whether having conversations or engaging in activities, can strengthen the bond.

5. **Physical touch**

We are showing love through physical gestures, like holding hands and gentle touches. Physical connection is important for those who feel loved through touch.

Dear new parents,
Take this with you and discover yours and your partner's love language or languages through conversations.
Make a conscious effort to express love that most resonates with your partner. This might seem small, but it can make a big difference to your loved ones.

Encourage each other to share your feelings, needs, and wants in an open chat to create mutual understanding.

REVIEWS FOR TEACHING BABY TO SLEEP

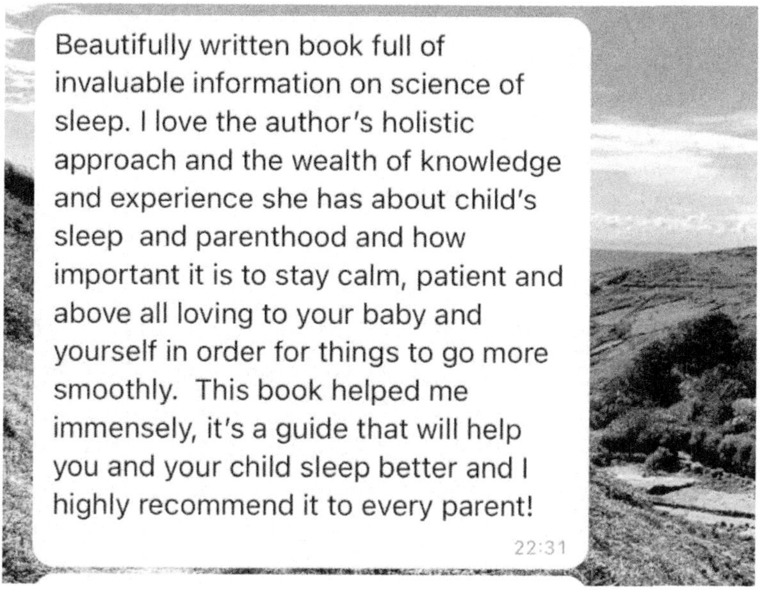
Beautifully written book full of invaluable information on science of sleep. I love the author's holistic approach and the wealth of knowledge and experience she has about child's sleep and parenthood and how important it is to stay calm, patient and above all loving to your baby and yourself in order for things to go more smoothly. This book helped me immensely, it's a guide that will help you and your child sleep better and I highly recommend it to every parent!

22:31

Marijana Novak

"It made things feel quite real and raw again and it was quite uncomfortable thinking back to that phase. But it's not only important to go back and remember those days for myself but also to share these stories so that other mums in a similar situation know they're not the only ones."

Client Comment

"Just by reading Ines's book, I learned things I didn't know in a way that was easy to understand. I appreciate how Ines breaks down sleep routines and explains how to create the perfect sleep environment for babies, as well as the hormones responsible for quality sleep and wake times.
Understanding this made it clear to me how important it is to start introducing bedtime routines for babies. I highly recommend this book to any new parent or caregiver looking to establish healthy sleep habits for their child— Ines's guidance is practical, insightful, and easy to follow."

Enia Monteiro

About the Author

Ines Zdelar is a family sleep coach and author with over 25 years of experience in childcare. Her journey into sleep coaching began with her own experience of sleep deprivation while working night shifts as a maternity nurse. This inspired her to explore the science of sleep and develop a deep understanding of the challenges new parents face.

Originally from Croatia, Ines moved to the UK at the age of 18, driven by her passion for working with children. Her extensive career has included working as a nanny with numerous families, teaching swimming, and gaining hands-on experience in Montessori settings. These roles have allowed her to connect with children of all ages and understand the importance of fostering confidence, independence, and a sense of security from an early age.

Ines firmly believes in the philosophy of "start them early." By introducing gentle sleep habits from the beginning, parents can provide their children with a strong foundation for navigating life's transitions with ease. Early routines help ensure that by the age of one, sleep becomes second nature, allowing families to cruise through challenges with confidence and harmony. Her approach emphasizes patience, consistency, and trust in the process, helping families build healthy sleep habits.

Her book, Teaching Baby to Sleep: The Ultimate Guide to Building Good Sleeping Habits from Birth to One Year, is a warm and practical guide designed to empower parents with step-by-step strategies for establishing healthy sleep routines. Ines's nurturing approach ensures parents feel supported while giving them the tools they need to succeed.

A passionate traveler, Ines draws inspiration from exploring the world, immersing herself in new cultures, and observing how families approach sleep across the globe. She loves discovering how different we all are, yet how universally essential rest is for connection and growth.

When she's not coaching or writing, Ines enjoys walking in nature, sharing coffee with loved ones, and finding inspiration in the beauty of everyday moments. Her dedication to helping families thrive shines through every page, offering parents the guidance and encouragement to create a happier, well-rested home.

Printed in Great Britain
by Amazon

53775377R00106